THE JOY RESET

SIX WAYS TRAUMA STEALS HAPPINESS
AND HOW TO GET IT BACK

BY MARYCATHERINE McDONALD, PhD

balance

New York   Boston

Balance
Hachette Book Group
1290 Avenue of the Americas
New York, NY 10104
GCP-Balance.com
@GCPBalance

First Edition: May 2025

Balance is an imprint of Grand Central Publishing. The Balance name and logo are registered trademarks of Hachette Book Group, Inc.

The publisher is not responsible for websites (or their content) that are not owned by the publisher.

Balance books may be purchased in bulk for business, educational, or promotional use. For information, please contact your local bookseller or the Hachette Book Group Special Markets Department at special.markets@hbgusa.com.

Print book interior design by Amy Quinn.

Library of Congress Cataloging-in-Publication Data

Names: McDonald, MaryCatherine, 1981– author.
Title: The joy reset : six ways trauma steals happiness and how to get it back / by MaryCatherine McDonald, PhD.
Description: First edition. | New York : Balance, 2025. | Includes bibliographical references and index.
Identifiers: LCCN 2024056018 | ISBN 9780306836268 (trade paperback) | ISBN 9780306836275 (ebook)
Subjects: LCSH: Joy. | Psychic trauma. | Psychic trauma—Alternative treatment. | Self-actualization (Psychology)
Classification: LCC BF575.H27 M3964 2025 | DDC 152.4/2—dc23/eng/20250212
LC record available at https://lccn.loc.gov/2024056018

ISBNs: 978-0-306-83626-8 (trade paperback), 978-0-306-83627-5 (ebook)

Printed in the United States of America

LSC-C

Printing 1, 2025

Listen, joy is coming.
Yes, even for you.

Contents

Author's Note: About the Stories in This Book   vii

Preface   ix

Chapter 1:
You're Joking, Right?
1

PART 1—Joy Resistance

Chapter 2:
Hypervigilance: Doves in the Prison Yard
33

Chapter 3:
Emotional Numbing: Making Meaning
in the Meaninglessness
61

PART 2—Joy Fear

Chapter 4:
Fear of Loss: Building Your Hope Circuit
93

Chapter 5:
Fear Conditioning: Joy When Joy Is Triggering
113

Contents

Chapter 6:
Joy for When You Don't Believe in Joy
145

PART 3—Joy Shame

Chapter 7:
Joy Guilt
169

Chapter 8:
Joy Shame
189

Epilogue
211

Acknowledgments 223

Notes 227

Index 229

Author's Note: About the Stories in This Book

The client stories presented in this book are composites. I've carefully changed all names and identifying details to protect the privacy and safety of those I work with. The examples you'll read here are not taken from any single client's story. Instead, they're inspired by common patterns and real issues that I've encountered over the years. My hope is that these stories honor the experiences of those I support, while offering you clarity, connection, and guidance in your own journey.

Preface

This book is a reintroduction to joy and hope.

But not the kind of joy and hope you might be thinking.

Not the kind of joy that floats around, soft and fluffy, like a pastel-colored balloon at a child's third birthday party. Not the kind of joy that dismisses your pain by telling you, "When life gives you lemons, make lemonade!" and insists that every moment sparkle. That's not joy; it's fear trying to shape-shift.

Joy is sinewy, fibrous, raw. Joy embraces the present moment and can hold opposing emotions together like nobody else. She has the audacity to interrupt you in the middle of your pity party and shout a rainbow across the floor as if to say, "Keep crying if you want, but *look!*" She jabs you with her elbow in the middle of your father's funeral and tells you a joke so inappropriate and hilarious that you have to hide your laughing face with your hanky.

And not the kind of hope that lives in an Instagram square and reminds you every morning that you "attract what you project." Not the kind of hope that sits over the kitchen counter and tells you in the "live, laugh, love" font that there is a "silver lining in every cloud." That's not hope; it's bullshit dressed in its Sunday best.

Hope is gritty. Glinting. Rebellious. Relentless. Hope

looks like she might be losing in the eleventh round, but she doesn't seem to notice. She is wiping blood off her face, dragging herself back to her feet, ears ringing, smirking, pulling her fists up for another round.

Joy and hope are fraternal twins, and they are not fucking around. They are here to meet you in the deepest, darkest depths—even when you don't want them there. They don't just know how to navigate the darkness; the darkness is their home. It's where they find their light. Joy is here to ground you in the present moment, and hope is here to help you keep an eye on the horizon.

Do you remember learning about the formation of stalactites and stalagmites? I know—it rings a bell, but that bell is way back in fourth grade sitting next to the tetherball court, so it's a little faint. Let me ring it for you again.

The whole absurd miracle begins with tiny droplets of water that seep through cracks and crevices in a cave ceiling. Once the water finds itself on the cave ceiling, it succumbs to the force of gravity and starts to drop to the cave floor. But it doesn't just drop. Each droplet contains dissolved minerals that have been gathered along its journey, and while it hangs from the ceiling waiting for gravity to become strong enough to pull it to the ground, some of those minerals get left behind. Over time, the repeated dripping and deposition of minerals result in the gradual growth of a hanging cylindrical structure. The stalactite extends downward as each new droplet adds another layer of minerals.

Remember this image: a mineral column creating itself out of almost nothing, and then reaching, reaching. This is hope, doing what should be absolutely impossible and gathering resources while she does it.

That wild alchemy of water to cylinder is only half the story. As the droplets hit the cave floor, they also leave behind a tiny deposit of minerals. Over time, these mineral deposits accumulate and grow upward, reaching for the very spot that they dripped from. These pillars are stalagmites. And this image? This is joy, taking the present moment and reaching up toward her sister, hope. Given enough time, stalactites and stalagmites—hope and joy—can meet and merge, forming a pillar, slowly and impossibly growing in the dark.

Just as water droplets gradually accumulate and form stalactites, hope always finds the cracks and crevices in the darkest of moments. Without our intervention, hope drips with relentless promise of better days, nourishing the growth of tiny moments of joy that rise right up from the floor of the cave—in this case the pain cave of your mind.

If water droplets can perform this absurd alchemical miracle, so can we.

Here's what I hope to do in this book. I want to make the kind of joy and hope that I've just been describing so unrelentingly clear to you that you notice it everywhere. In a world full of din and darkness, it can be all too easy to miss tiny pieces of glinting mica. But they are here. I also want to show you that not only are they here, but they are also not opposed to the dark. Joy does not exist only in the moments that are free of pain. That's a false story. In fact, the brightest, tiniest, most important pieces can be found *only* in the dark. Once you can't help but notice it, I want to teach you how to harness and amplify the power of that glinting magic—because this sustainable, endless light source will do more than help you get through your darkest, scariest, loneliest times. It will also rewire your brain.

Along the way, I'm going to introduce you to the six thieves of joy and hope. These thieves are partners in crime with trauma, and whether you're aware of it or not, you're probably familiar with some of them. Maybe all of them. These thieves stand ready and waiting to steal your joy and hope at every chance. They stand at your front door and make sure that joy and hope either do not get in at all, or if they do happen to sneak in, they get thrown right back out. We need to bring these thieves all the way into the light so we can figure out how to outsmart them. Because here's the thing about thieves: their whole game depends on your not being able to navigate the dark as well as they can. That means all we have to do is get to know their darkness, and we can beat them. There are six of them, but they're not as brilliantly unique as they might think. In fact, without even knowing it, they've organized themselves into three categories: resistance, fear, and shame.

Joy resistance happens when trauma whispers in our ear that these happier emotions are so ridiculous that they're probably not even real. Here we have two thieves—hypervigilance and emotional numbing—standing at the door, refusing to even let hope and joy in. Not even a sliver. They've drawn the shades, and when joy and hope knock at the door, they push them back down the front steps. "Joy? Hope? Nope. Not for me. Are these things even real?" Door slam.

Joy fear happens when trauma has taught us that positive experiences and feelings are illusions—false promises that trick us into thinking that truly terrible things are *not* just around the corner. Then we get clobbered. How humiliating. Worry not! These two thieves—fear of loss and fear conditioning—stand ready to remind you. "Joy? Hope? No. No, no, no, no, no. We have seen these two fools before. We've even let them in. Remember what happened next? Yeah. That. Never again." Door slam.

Joy guilt or joy shame happens when our traumatic experiences trick us into thinking that our job here on earth is to feel bad *forever*. They do this by telling us that if we move on, we are betraying someone or something, ensuring that the first blush of joy quickly flashes into embarrassment and dread. These two thieves are nearly identical twins—you know, the kind that trick each other's teachers by switching schedules. What starts out as guilt—am I really feeling OK after this awful thing?—can morph seamlessly into shame: if I'm really feeling OK after this awful thing, I must be a bad person. We'll call this category "joy shame," because shame is the stronger and louder twin. "Hope and joy? Pfft. Maybe those are things other people can have, but us? We're not worthy." Door slam.

You might have one of these thieves, or you might have all six. But now, you also have me, and I am not afraid of these thieves. I've been watching them for years, and I know all their moves. I've built you tools and exercises designed specifically to banish each one. So go get your spelunking gear, and let's head to the caves; we've got work to do.

Hey, listen. Before we get started, I have an important note.

This is a dark little book about joy. I really mean it when I say that the joy and hope you find here are gritty. We're going to talk about grief, violence, suicide. These things might be upsetting. I wouldn't have put them here for you if I didn't think they were going to help, but if you find yourself overwhelmed at any point—by the stories or the tools—here is your permission slip to take a huge break. Skip bits. Put the book down. Throw it across the room. Only you can decide what works for you and when.

Be gentle with yourself.

CHAPTER 1

You're Joking, Right?

Life is a shipwreck, but we must not
forget to sing in the lifeboats.

—Voltaire

"JOY? JOY. JOY! ARE YOU FUCKING SERIOUS? I DON'T have time for fucking joy! Aren't you fucking listening? Have you managed to understand a single aspect of my life? Joy. You know what? Go fuck yourself."

And with that, my client Christina snapped her computer closed, abruptly ending our Zoom session. I tried bringing hope and joy to my practice. Given the treacly treatment that hope and joy almost always get, I probably should not have been surprised that Christina told me to fuck off after I tried to prescribe her this three-letter word.

Picture this: It's late in the summer of 2020—the height

of the COVID-19 pandemic. Lockdowns, travel restrictions, social distancing. Economic disruptions, job losses, and a healthcare system buckling under the pressure of it all. A global movement against racial injustice and police brutality sparked by the killing of George Floyd. An economic downturn wringing out the global economy, devastating families and households.

I was seeing eight to nine clients a day in addition to teaching full time and writing two books. In between things, I was searching frantically through the research for new interventions that might help my clients. So many of them were struggling with multiple awful things at the same time, and even with an extensive trauma background, I still didn't feel properly resourced. What we were living through was, literally, unprecedented.

And then I read about the hope circuit. To give you a quick snapshot—we'll go much more into detail in Chapter 4—the hope circuit is a powerful neural network within our brains that fuels optimism, resilience, and a sense of possibility. It is a complex interplay of brain regions that wire together, almost like a circuit board. When activated, this circuitry generates feelings of anticipation, motivation, and belief in positive change. It helps us envision a better future, set goals, and take action toward achieving them. Activating the hope circuit enables us to overcome obstacles, rebound from setbacks, and maintain a positive outlook even in challenging times. Pretty cool, right? I thought so too. By understanding and nurturing this circuit, we can harness its potential to inspire and propel us forward on our journey.

How do you activate the hope circuit? It's actually really simple. Through regular practice of gratitude, hope, and joy. Seriously?! Yep. Seriously. I dug all the way into the research and started teaching classes, groups, and clients about the hope circuit. And we started practicing together. And it was working. Mostly. Except with Christina.

It's 6:30 p.m. on a Friday, and Christina is Zooming from her bed. She is so full of simmering rage that I'm starting to worry she's going to have a heart attack. We've been working together for about three months, and the needle won't budge. Not one iota. Christina hates her coworkers—they are incompetent. She can't stand her husband—an unemployed loser who doesn't listen. Her friends don't have a "single fucking clue"—about how hard it is for her. Neither does her ailing, pathetic father—actually, no one does!

Christina's vitriol is visceral and seemingly bottomless. There's a ton of energy behind it, but it is not a sustainable fuel source, and what I don't think she sees is how destructive it is. It's been three months, and I have never seen her smile, never heard her laugh. There is nothing good about the world, nothing good about her life, nothing good about anything. None of this current stuff is what Christina thinks she came to see me for. She came to see me to sort through some childhood trauma, but she is frustrated that we never get to dig into that because she's got so much current rage to burn through. I tell her that her rage is relevant and informing her daily life, so it's not wasted time by any means, but the irritation at her husband and everything else in her life is a symptom, and we need to go to the source. But there is just too much to wade through, and she is stuck and I am stuck and then, I have an idea.

I start telling her about posttraumatic growth, which is the fact—not the hypothesis, the *fact*—that individuals who go through traumatic events often undergo incredible positive psychological transformations. Transformations that they would not have gone through without the trauma. I tell her about the research in positive psychology—and how if we can figure out how to turn her dials to gratitude and hope, she will start to feel differently about the world and her place in it. I tell her about the hope circuit and that I think she needs to be open to the experience of joy in order to heal.

And with that, Christina slams her laptop shut, and the session—and our relationship—is done. I am baffled for a few minutes, but it does not take long for me to see what I had done. I had accidentally dismissed her entirely. It was as if I had said to Christina, "Look, it's simple! All we need to do is get to a place where you can feel some hope for that dark swirling abyss that is your future, some gratitude for your neglectful and needy husband, and some appreciation for the resilience you developed in your unfair and brutal childhood." It was like I was asking her to jump directly into the sea without any swimming lessons. I would have told me to go fuck myself too. Although hope and joy are positive emotions, this does not mean that the way we feel about them is always positive. We needed to scale down— way down—and maybe start by first just locating joy. Did it ever exist? What was it like? What happened to it, and where did it go?

I wrote Christina a long email the next day, apologizing and trying to explain why I had thought this obviously ill-timed discussion might help. I tried to point out the research—how solid it was, how well it was working with some of my groups and other clients. But it didn't help. I had broken her trust, made her feel unheard, deployed the exact wrong intervention at the exact wrong moment.

What Christina doesn't know is that she helped so many other clients after her, because she made me see that her resistance has something critical to add to the conversation. Yes, the research shows—unequivocally—that gratitude, hope, and joy can rewire the brain and nervous system. And. Just like any intervention that aims to heal, the way that it is deployed matters. A lot. Trying to get someone to lean into these things at the wrong time is like trying to get your grass to grow by driving a truck all over it.

I'm still sorry I missed that step with Christina. So, I'm going to take her cue and start here in the weeds of doubt. Before we dive in and start practicing and rewiring and finding hope and joy, let's make sure that we know what kind of barriers we might encounter so we can navigate around them when we need to. The first barrier for me is always buy-in. Why should I care about these positive emotions precisely when I'm not feeling them? Let's dig into the research for just a moment.

WHY JOY? WHY HOPE?

Positive psychology emerged in the 1990s with an aim to shift the focus of psychological research from solely studying mental illness and dysfunction to understanding human well-being and flourishing. What would happen if we investigated positive emotions rather than just pathology? In what way did character strength impact someone's overall well-being? Where did qualities like grit and resilience come from, and how could they be reinforced and cultivated? How might we unravel someone's patterns of fear and withdrawal?

With these questions in hand, researchers set off and conducted studies to examine the effects of positive emotions on overall well-being. Two key emotions came out of this research and became pillars of flourishing. If you can get and maintain these two things, you can conquer all. What are these two mainstays of psychological health, you ask? Gratitude and hope.

Gratitude—which is essentially the emotion that comes from imprinting joyful moments or experiences—emerged as a key emotion associated with various positive outcomes. Over and over again, studies revealed that simple practices like keeping gratitude journals, writing thank-you notes, and engaging in acts of kindness increased life satisfaction and reduced symptoms of depression and anxiety.

Researchers investigated the concept of hope and its impact on people's lives. Studies examined how hope influences goal setting, motivation, coping with adversity, and overall psychological health. They found that individuals with higher levels of hope demonstrated greater resilience, goal attainment, and subjective well-being.

Building on these sparkling research findings, positive psychology honed evidence-based therapeutic interventions to promote these positive emotions of gratitude and hope. These interventions included gratitude exercises, goal-setting techniques, cognitive restructuring to foster positive thinking, and positive future visualization.

Are you rolling your eyes yet? I know.

As an interdisciplinary researcher whose job is specifically to think critically about the field of psychology in general, I must tell you candidly that I completely dismissed the subfield of positive psychology until recently. I thought it was a Pollyanna-ish nicety that came out of the '90s and had really limited applications if you were facing actual distress, trauma, or dysfunction. But then I looked more deeply into the science.

I wanted to see whether any of these shiny, happy results were long-term, and whether they appeared across multiple studies, so I looked for longitudinal studies and meta-analyses. These studies follow individuals over extended periods and combine data from multiple studies to provide comprehensive analyses. When psychologists do this, they are looking to answer two questions: First, what are all these independent studies actually showing? And second, does the effect they are claiming have sustainability—are the patients truly getting better and staying better? What I found was that studies consistently—basically always—supported the positive effects of gratitude and hope on well-being, relationships, resilience, and personal growth.

And then came the neuroscience.

Neuroimaging research came about in the late 1990s, which made it possible for researchers to study brain activity noninvasively. They did this using functional magnetic resonance imaging, or fMRI, which allows you to see blood flow and brain activity in real time. In the 2000s, neuroimaging studies began to emerge showing that positive emotion and well-being really were neurally connected—meaning that practicing things like daily gratitude exercises could actually change blood flow in the brain, regulating the nervous system from the top down, and in turn increasing overall happiness, contentment, and function.

Check this out. In one study, participants were divided into three groups, and all participants kept a journal for ten weeks. One group was instructed to write down things they were grateful for. The second group recorded daily hassles and irritations. The third group listed neutral events. Researchers found that participants in the gratitude group reported significantly higher levels of subjective well-being and life satisfaction compared to the other two groups. Not only that, but fMRI scans also revealed that the gratitude group showed greater activation in the medial prefrontal cortex, a brain region associated with reward processing and positive emotions. The takeaway here? Gratitude practice changes your mood on a *neurobiological level* by modulating blood flow and electrical activity in your brain.[1]

What about hope?

Glad you asked. In a study that aimed to examine the relationship between hope and mental health in older adults, participants were assessed for hope levels and then followed up over a four-year period to measure their mental health outcomes. The study found that higher levels of hope were associated with better mental health outcomes in older adults. Additionally, fMRI scans revealed that individuals with higher levels of hope exhibited greater activation in the prefrontal cortex and other brain regions associated with positive affect (i.e., all the parts that are responsible for the experience of pleasant emotions and mood) and cognitive control. Again, these findings suggest that hope involves cognitive and emotional processes that influence mental well-being.[2]

From a research perspective, the positive impact of gratitude and hope was getting harder and harder to roll my eyes at. But as a practitioner working with clients facing trauma, and as an individual working through my own trauma, I was still solidly on the fence. Hope and gratitude can feel absurdly, impossibly hard to reach when the foundation of the world has just shattered underneath your feet.

Gratitude? For what? After trauma, the world feels uninhabitable, and the only emotion that feels accessible is the panic that rips through your body as if someone jammed a grenade in your mouth and pulled the pin. Hope for the future? Try glancing into the once glimmering and expansive future that you used to be able to visualize so easily. In the midst of trauma, it is more than likely that you will be met with a howling and terrifying abyss. This is the puzzle, then—how do we get to joy and hope when we're plummeting through the darkness?

SIX WAYS TRAUMA STEALS JOY

Let's start by getting on the same page in terms of trauma. This is a word with a storied past and a confusing present.

Each and every one of us arrives here with a set of default trauma responses. You've probably heard of these: fight, flight, and freeze (hang on, I'll get to fawn in a second). These responses are thought to have evolved over time to keep us safe—they are emergency coping mechanisms that kick in if and only if we are sufficiently overwhelmed to need them.

Each of these responses does something different to help us out when we are in danger. Fight helps us kick and scream when our system has decided we're facing an enemy that we can probably conquer. Flight helps us get the hell out of Dodge when our system has decided that we might not be able to fight, but we can get away. And freeze helps us disconnect from ourselves when we cannot fight and cannot get away.

A quick note on fawn and other *f* words that get added to the list: you can develop more sophisticated trauma responses based on experience and conditioning. Fawn is one of these. It is a very real trauma response whereby an abused person learns how to calm and coddle their abuser to avoid further (or worse) abuse. Since fawn involves learning—how to anticipate the moods of an abuser, how to calm them down—I do not include it in the group of default trauma responses that we share with babies and lizards. Why? It's important to distinguish the default responses from the ones that we learn, because if we lump them all together, we run the risk of missing important information. For example, if I show up as an adult who fawns, *and* we know that I didn't show up on earth with that response as a part of my default wiring, that means *I learned that somewhere*. Where I learned it and how can be crucial pieces of information that I need in order to process and heal.

It's critical to understand that each of these responses gets chosen for us by our nervous systems and in milliseconds. When we are sufficiently overwhelmed and potentially in danger, our rational mind does not choose what comes next; our nervous system does.

One crucial little piece we need to understand here is that when the trauma responses are going off in the brain and body, other things are necessarily shut down to preserve energy. Chief among the things that are shut down are the parts of the brain we use to rationally think through things and create organized and accessible memories (the prefrontal cortex and the hippocampus). The result is that post trauma, we end up with fragmented memories that can give way to all sorts of symptoms. Trauma is primarily a disease of memory.

Alright. So what kinds of things set off the trauma response? What kinds of things are traumatic? Well, we know that we've evolved to have these emergency coping mechanisms. And we have also evolved to love a list, so it's only natural that we are tempted to create a list of potentially traumatic experiences. "Look!" we say. "Here is the comprehensive list of all the things that can be traumatic! Now we can simply avoid them." Not so fast—there are a couple of problems with this method. First of all, lists are something that the *mind* makes; decisions about threat are something that the *body* makes. There are bound to be mistakes when we set out to ignore the wisdom of the body. Second, and related, *literally anything* can be traumatic given the right set of circumstances. What would be much more helpful is to base our definition of trauma in *how an event takes hold of the nervous system* rather than *what the event is*.

In light of that, here's the definition I use. Anytime you are exposed to something that is overwhelming enough to cause the emergency systems (fight, flight, and freeze) to kick into gear, you've been exposed to something traumatic. What seems to decide whether that trauma will wedge itself into your psyche and soul is whether you've got a supportive person (or several) that can help you process what was too overwhelming to process in the moment. I call that a relational home.

Let's recap the three things we've covered so far. First, default trauma responses (fight, flight, freeze) are hardwired. Second, when these responses kick in, it means we have been exposed to trauma, full stop. Doesn't matter if the exposure is coming from sexual assault or being humiliated by your boss. Third, to prevent traumatic exposure from turning into lasting trauma, and in order to heal lasting trauma, we need a relational home.

What does this have to do with joy and hope? Let's zoom out just a bit and think about how repetitive exposure to trauma can shape a developing human. In addition to arriving on earth with trauma responses, and loving lists, humans are also *miraculously* adaptive. We are shaped and conditioned by *all* our experiences. Our brains and bodies imprint what we go through and organize our memories so that we can navigate the world more safely. The more I remember, the more likely I am to stay alive.

We are perhaps never as malleable as we are when we are most vulnerable—from ages zero to eighteen. During this time, the developing brain absorbs experiences and shapes its neural pathways accordingly, *rapidly* forming connections based on the environment and interactions. This changes the way that we understand and engage with the world. Think about a child who finds out that if she learns how to read, she will get *gold stars* in school (OK, it's me). Whenever I get a gold star, my brain releases a quick little blast of dopamine, which is a neurotransmitter associated with pleasure and reward. The more I repeat this, the stronger the neural connections become between reading and positive feelings. My gold-star-starved little brain starts associating reading with reward, and over time I develop a love for reading. Put another way: What do I learn? Reading equals warm, fuzzy feeling. What do I do? *Keep reading.* (Even without the gold stars, which I regret to tell you I haven't gotten in a *very* long time.)

The malleability of the brain is crucial for learning and development, but it doesn't just imprint the gold stars and positive learning experiences. To ensure that we survive, it prioritizes negative lessons of fear and danger. This is called fear conditioning, which is a form of associative learning where a neutral stimulus becomes quickly associated with a frightening event, leading to an automatic and intense fear response. Fear conditioning plays a *major* role in mapping the developing brain. If you forget about gold stars, you might read less, but if you forget that bears are not friendly even though they are fuzzy, you might make a fatal mistake. This prioritizing of negative experiences is protective by design, but it can have profound and lasting impacts.

Think about a child who is frequently scolded or punished harshly for making small mistakes or expressing emotions. Each time that child is punished, the fear center of the brain (the amygdala) lights up and sends messages to the memory center (the hippocampus) that tell us we'd better encode these experiences as dangerous so we can make sure to avoid them in the future. In addition to that, since the brain is still in early development, it doesn't have a lot of capacity to modulate emotions. (Have you ever witnessed a toddler spontaneously regulating themselves out of a tantrum? Me neither.) The only other available way to cope is to avoid them. What does that child learn? Making mistakes and expressing emotions equals all kinds of trouble. What does that child do? Avoid situations where they might make a mistake or show an inconvenient emotion. If we're not careful, we can get a whole life built on a pattern of fear and withdrawal.

What's critical to understand is that this pattern of avoidance doesn't limit itself to negative experiences. Over time, our nervous system can come to treat even positive emotions—like hope and joy—with the same caution. These emotions, though we might cognitively understand that they are good, may start to feel risky if we've learned that reaching for something bright often comes with a sting. Although hope and joy are positive emotions, this does not mean that the way we feel about them is always positive. If we have trauma in our background, we can respond to hope and joy as if they are dangerous. Taking Christina's cue, I want to normalize this and help us to understand why positive emotions can be so difficult.

Hope and joy can both trigger intense opposition, especially for folks who have a history of trauma. It's critical to understand that this opposition is not a flaw in the system; it's an attempt at adaptation. When we have traumatic experiences, our brains and bodies learn to brace against the world as a way to protect us. This completely makes sense. In fact, it's genius. How else would you learn to avoid a hot stove, poisonous mushrooms, or unemployed musicians with motorcycles? But sometimes our systems get *too* protective. Like a well-meaning but overprotective parent, sometimes this bracing can backfire and end up protecting us from the wrong things.

There are (at least) six reasons—yes, here come the thieves—that you might be wary of these fraternal twin emotions of hope and joy. Let's sketch these out in some detail so we can learn to notice when they show up. As I mentioned in the preface, they're organized into three categories: joy resistance, joy fear, and joy shame.

Joy Resistance

#1. Hypervigilance

People who have experienced trauma often live in a state of hypervigilance, where they are constantly on alert for potential threat. This might look like not being able to sleep at night and walking the perimeter of the house as if it's a battle zone, or feeling like you have to manage the emotional response of everyone in any room that you are in, or feeling like you might crawl out of your skin if you must sit with your back to an open restaurant. Positive emotions like joy or hope lower this state of alertness, which can lead to a sense of vulnerability. When you are experiencing a trauma trigger or dealing with trauma chronically, the fear center in your brain is like a sniper—laser focused and never sleeping. That sniper needs to stay alert, alive. Hope and joy? These are not simply a luxury; they are fatal distractions. So, avoiding positive emotions can be a way to maintain your sense of safety.

#2. Emotional Numbing

When we haven't fully processed the emotions from past traumas, we tend to suppress or avoid *all* emotions over time because it protects us from becoming overwhelmed. We numb in various ways—we might avoid music or movies that will make us feel something, or chronically reach for distractions to get us through the day, or lean on substances like drugs and alcohol to block out intense feelings and experiences. It's important to understand that when we do this, we often do so compulsively—out of desperation. We don't wake up in the morning and think, "I'd like to feel numb today!" Something in our subconscious pulls an emergency lever so we can continue to function. The thing is, our brains are not great at selective numbing because that isn't very efficient. So, if we are numbing anything, we end up numbing everything. This can help protect us against anxiety and terror but will also result in a reduced ability to experience joy or feel hope for the future.

Joy Fear

#3. Fear of Loss

If you have experienced trauma, you are acutely attuned to the precarity of happiness. It may be here now, but it could all disappear and be replaced by tragedy in an instant, in a nanosecond. You know that because you've lived it. You've sat there in shock, eyes as wide as Saturn's rings. And then you've had to wrestle not only with the loss, but with the fact that you didn't see it coming. You were left humiliated because you got lulled into thinking that things would be OK this time. Never again. No way. I can't predict what's going to happen to me, but I can avoid looking like a total sucker. Fear of loss can be a six-mile-high wall sitting between you and positive emotions.

#4. Conditioning

Ever since 1920, when Dr. John Watson made Little Albert afraid of a harmless white rat by pairing the appearance of the rat with an upsetting loud noise, researchers have been fascinated with how quickly fear can be conditioned in the brain. We now know that when fear gets tied to a stimulus, it's an especially strong tie—titanium strong. If you have had positive emotions in a situation that quickly turned traumatic, you might have unconsciously paired fear with those positive emotions. To your brain, joy is Little Albert's white rat—something you used to love that now makes you quiver in fear.

Joy Shame

#5. Guilt

Survivors of trauma can feel guilt for experiencing joy for many reasons. The emotions can feel ill-fitting and inappropriate given the circumstances. Almost like showing up to a party in full costume only to find out it wasn't a costume party after all. How can you reconcile laughing at a sitcom just days after your friend dies of brain cancer at thirty-four? How can you feel joy at getting your dream job if your city has just been through a terrorist attack? These feelings can seem inappropriate, unfair, taboo. Guilt steals positive emotions from us. It tricks us into thinking that the only way we can restore justice is if we continue to feel bad.

#6. Shame

Shame is like the emperor of these thieves, the final boss. As you probably know all too well, trauma can profoundly impact your sense of self-worth. After trauma, many people internalize the belief that they are fundamentally damaged, broken, and unworthy. Though it may sound counterintuitive, it is often easier to get our heads around the idea that the terrible thing that happened is all our fault than it is to admit that the world can be terrifying. "There must be something wrong with me" gives you the locus of control and the belief that if you can figure out the wrong thing about you and fix it, you will be protected from future pain. The side effect is that this line of thinking can make positive emotions feel like something you don't deserve even if they are standing right there in front of you, purring and batting their eyelashes.

We'll get to know each of these thieves and learn how to banish them throughout the course of this book. For now, I want to validate the opposition: There is *nothing* wrong with you if you avoid or sabotage joy. You are not dark or bad or broken. In fact, know that if you find yourself avoiding joy, there are *at least* six possible reasons that you would do that. Six reasons that are grounded in your very real past. Six reasons that make a whole lot of sense.

I started with Christina to give you an idea of what barriers might get in our way. Now, I want to share a joy success story, so we know what life looks like at the summit. You want to know what the view looks like before you get to it so you can make sure it's photogenic and worth all the sweat, right? I can promise you until I'm blue in the face that it is this time, but maybe it's just better to give you a glimpse of your own.

JOY IN THE PSYCH WARD

I love working with Lena. She is engaged, curious, totally connected, and trusting. She's willing to look at difficult things, knows to pause, and doesn't hold back any important details. She's not testing me or wasting time. We are *in it* from the first thirty seconds to the fifty-minute mark every session. Which is good because she has a lot of shit to figure out.

Each week we had been gently exploring the end of her marriage. We discussed the ways in which her partnership was not fulfilling, ways in which her husband had perhaps been taking advantage of Lena's willingness, ways in which she was being emotionally abused. These are delicate topics that no one wants to talk about—especially when the subjects are in their actual lives and not in a TV show or movie. But Lena was committed to the climb. Realizing with each step that what was going on was not acceptable. Thinking about ways that she could pick up the next stone in the path and start heading in a different direction. We talked often and gently about joy and hope. About how her relationship had conditioned her into fearing love, how trauma was tricking her into thinking she was not capable or deserving of a healthy relationship. We were getting to know which thieves were standing in between her and happiness and learning how to outsmart them.

It is also worth noting that Lena is very tethered to reality. She's reflective and aware of herself, her emotions, and what's happening. Not once in my years of working with her did I worry about delusion or psychosis. This will make sense shortly. When she comes in for our session that Friday, she looks fired up, ready to go.

"Boy, do I have a story for you," she starts.

"Uh oh . . ." I say, trying quickly to parse her facial expression. She is sitting a little straighter than usual, and she looks pale, like she has seen a ghost.

"Well, let's see. To start, I spent seventy-two hours in the psych ward this week."

"Wait. *What?*" I immediately start doing psychological calculus in my head. Had I missed something big? I flash back to our previous session, which had been only a week ago. It had been tough, but not terribly intense. We had laughed a little, even. What did I miss? She told me about the plans she had with her daughters that weekend. We talked about movies they were going to see. What on earth had happened in the space of less than seven days that landed Lena in a psych ward?

It turns out that in a draconian move of epic proportions, her soon-to-be ex-husband had her committed on false pretenses. In most states, an individual can be detained for mental health evaluation if they are deemed a danger to themselves or others, or if they are gravely disabled due to a mental disorder. During the hold, mental health professionals assess the person's condition to determine if further treatment or hospitalization is needed. After seventy-two hours, the individual must either be released, agree to voluntary treatment, or be placed under a longer hold with court approval. Lena was not at all a danger to herself or others, nor was she gravely disabled due to her mental health—but her ex-husband had claimed that she was. You likely already know this, but the psych ward is not, like, a pleasant place to be in. If you're there against your will, you will naturally want to spend every waking minute explaining to the doctors and nurses that this has all been a big mistake—that you really don't need to be there. The problem is that's exactly what someone would say who *did* need to be there. So, you have to show them that it's a mistake. You have to show them that you are tethered to reality all while feeling trapped, like a beetle under a bell jar.

The first step? Accept it. You are here for seventy-two hours. That part is mandatory. This is a good place to say that though these forced stays sound terrible, they exist for a reason. They can be stabilizing and lifesaving for both the people admitted and those around them. But that was not the case for Lena. She was stable and not a danger to herself or others in any way. She was there and knew that she didn't need to be. Really quickly, she had to accept that this temporary stay was simply not going to end at twenty-four or even thirty-six hours. And then? She immediately turned to joy.

Yes, she was in the psych ward, and there was a beautiful cherry tree outside that she could look at.

Yes, she was in the psych ward, and there were mystery books that she could read all day long. She hadn't had a chance to read fiction in forever.

Yes, she was in the psych ward, *and* she could spend these few days teaching the other people in the ward about joy.

Yes, the cave, and yes, the stalactites and stalagmites.

Yes, the darkness, and yes, the light.

Wait. Did you see that part about Lena teaching the other patients about joy? That's exactly what she did. She used her seventy-two hours in the psych ward to teach twenty-four other people how to notice joy in the deepest of darks, how to find hope for a life that has no future. She used a practice that I taught her called tiny little joys. It's a very simple exercise where you try and notice small, joyful things that exist amid everything else in your life. It's a gloomy day as I'm writing this, for example, and I've got a perfect Americano sitting to the right of my laptop. The more you make yourself do this, the more joys you notice. In other words, you start to train your worldview to notice and imprint tiny little joys. Even in the shittiest times. It's a simple tool, and Lena explained it to anyone in the ward who would listen.

Your next question will be this: How did *that* go?

Lena's new friends grasped the tools she gave them immediately. They started shouting to each other about little joys when they found them.

"I LOVE THIS BLANKET!"

"JUDGE MATHIS IS ON!"

"LOOK AT THE SUNSET!"

"I FINISHED THIS BOOK AGAIN!"

When her time was up, Lena gave several of the other patients her cell phone number. A few months later, she had whoever was available to her house for Sunday dinner. They laughed and talked joy and Judge Mathis and had a great time. Three years later, she still gets daily joy texts from some of them.

Here's the takeaway: Yes, joy and hope might seem impossible to reach, and even harder to hold onto. Yes, you might have resistance. Your first thought when you picked up this book might have been pretty similar to Christina's. Joy? Seriously? How about you go fuck yourself. Yes, you might be afraid. Ashamed. And I promise you that these fraternal twins of brain rewiring are available to you, if you are open to them. I promise you that they will change your life.

If Lena and her buddies at the psych ward can do it, so can we.

QUICK HOPE AND JOY AUDIT

Let's take a moment and assess where you are exactly on the joy/hope spectrum. Many times, we have a visceral opinion—an intense reaction when we hear a word or phrase—but haven't unpacked that opinion to see what's there. When we do, we can get a whole lot of information about what barriers might come up for us.

One of the very best ways to figure out how we feel about something right now is to free write. This is when you use a prompt, set a timer, put pen to paper (or fingers to keyboard), and write without pause until the timer goes off. The goal here isn't to write something coherent, to think through what you are going to write for an hour, or to write for someone else's eyes. The goal is to connect to the subterranean part of your brain and let it tell you what it thinks.

Step 1) Set a timer for four minutes.

Step 2) Read aloud the word "joy."

Step 3) Write anything that comes to mind until the timer goes off.

Step 4) Repeat steps 1–3 for the word "hope."

Step 5) Step away for a little while and then read back what you've written. Take note of what surprises you. Did specific memories come up? Song lyrics? Poems that you had to memorize in ninth grade?

What emotions were sparked? Excitement? Anger? Boredom? None of this is to be judged, just noticed. Save this piece of paper to revisit when you're done with this book. You can repeat this exercise, then do a side-by-side comparison. How have your ideas about these emotions changed?

SCALING DOWN JOY—TINY LITTLE JOYS

There are two critical ways in which we get joy very, *very* wrong. First, we assume that in order to have any efficacy, joy has to be equal in size to the pain we have experienced. Have a terrible day? You need a day like Ferris Bueller's day off to bump out the dent it caused in your psyche. Second, we assume that the purpose of joy is to counter pain. That if it is real, authentic, bona fide joy, it will reverse the pain. Tip the seesaw to the other side. Neither of these is true, and I have much—much—more to say about that, but for now just know these two things:

- joy does not have to be equal in size to pain in order to count, and
- joy does not have to counter or solve the pain; it can just sit right there beside it.

In fact, I'll show you. Grab a piece of paper.

Step 1) Compost pile—On the bottom right side of the paper, draw a medium-size box and label it

"Compost." Then, inside the box, make a compost list. Write down every crappy thing that you are currently dealing with. It's Monday. Your office is cold. You have to go to the grocery store on the way home. You're still struggling with anxiety. You're in the middle of a divorce. You hate your haircut.

Step 2) Look for tiny little joys (TLJs)—Right now, look around you and find a handful of little things that give you a burst of happiness. These can be really small. It might be the feeling of your toes wiggling in your favorite socks, the postcard you have from a friend tacked up on the wall behind your desk, the shameless club banger playing from your playlist. It could be the way that the sun is streaming through the window right now and shining directly on your AT&T bill, the text you just got from your crush, or the fact that you're about to make your favorite dinner. Each time you discover one, start at the top of your page and write it down on your piece of paper.

Step 3) Imprint them—Now that you've got a list of current TLJs (three will do!), sit with them for a moment. Take ten to twenty seconds and think about them. Savor them. Close your eyes if you want. As you think about that little list of TLJs, notice what's happening in your body. Where is the joy taking hold? What is it doing? You might notice a release of

TINY LITTLE JOY TRACKER

MONDAY

TUESDAY

WEDNESDAY

THURSDAY

FRIDAY

SATURDAY

WEEKLY WINS

- ○ _____
- ○ _____
- ○ _____
- ○ _____
- ○ _____
- ○ _____
- ○ _____

SUNDAY

COMPOST

THE FIRST SIP OF COFFEE IN THE MORNING

tension, a soft, relaxed feeling in your face, warmth, goosebumps. *Anything* you notice, just feel into it, and try to extend the feeling for a half a second longer.

Step 4) Repeat—Like just about anything else in life, we can't just practice TLJs one time and call it done. Repeated and sustained practice is what is going to start creating major shifts in your mindset. Even here it's totally OK to start small. Try tracking one to three TLJs for a week and see what changes.

You might be wondering about the compost pile. Why start an exercise aimed at joy with a bunch of, well, crap? Two reasons. First, the crap is there, and the purpose of the joy is not to erase it, it's to sit beside it. This may sound like a small goal, but it's a radical reframing because we so often get tricked into thinking that the crap is *all there is*. That our traumas are the only things about us, or the most important things about us. That our mistakes shape our paths more than anything else we do. None of that is true. But sometimes we have to trick ourselves out of what we tricked ourselves into. And by placing the compost right next to the joy, we're tricking ourselves into seeing both. The goal here is not to eradicate the darkness from our lives. If we set that as our goal, we'll be setting ourselves up for failure. The goal is to figure out how to find and see the light when we are in the dark. To do this we have to acknowledge the existence of both. So, yes, the crap. And yes, the joy.

Second, we have to be careful to avoid a fate worse than any of the thieves: toxic positivity. Toxic positivity is the idea that the way to handle anything dark in life is to simply always maintain a positive mindset. You know positivity is toxic if it dismisses or avoids your real emotions. Lose your job in a shocking layoff? Stay positive! Did your beloved family pet just die? Look on the bright side! No more litter-box to clean! Death of a family member? They're in a better place! Oof, oof, oof. Toxic positivity occurs when positive thinking is pushed to an extreme, invalidating or dismissing real and often painful emotions that need to be acknowledged and processed. And that is *not* what we are doing here. The crap is here. The darkness is here. And so is the joy. So is the light. By putting them on the same page, what we are cuing our brains to realize is that it's not one or the other; it's always both.

OK. Now that we've oriented ourselves and acknowledged the opposition, it's time to go a little deeper into the cave. I've organized the rest of the book into three parts to correspond with the three categories of joy thieves. First category up? Resistance. Its thieves? Hypervigilance and emotional numbing.

PART 1

JOY
RESISTANCE

CHAPTER 2

Hypervigilance: Doves in the Prison Yard

There is no "them" and "us." There is only "us."

—Father Greg Boyle

FRANK IS MY FIRST SESSION OF THE DAY. IT'S ONLY 9:00 a.m., but I've got my blinds shut tight against the relentless Los Angeles sunshine. It bounces off the buildings and the concrete and the water and the windshields, and sometimes I sit in my closet just to get a break. It never rains here, and even when it's gray (a.k.a. June Gloom—you have to say that out loud and with a heavy vocal fry like a true Angelino), it's somehow still punishing. Frank and I alternate between in-person and phone sessions, and I'm grateful that this one is on the phone because it means I can close my eyes—one more shield against the sun. It pierces through anyway. Relentless.

Frank is doing really well. He's sweeping his room and chatting to his neighbors and roommates, and in between all of that he's telling me he just came in from buying break-fast sandwiches for some of the guys who live on the corner. "Feels good, MC, real good, to be on this side. You know?" He laughs. I smile. "I know it, Frank." Frank has this habit of saying my name every other sentence. I'm not sure if it's to make me feel special, or to make sure I'm really listening, or to add urgency, or because he read *The 7 Habits of Highly Effective People* too many times in prison. Whatever the rea-son, it's endearing, and I can't help doing it back just in case it helps him see that I am listening.

I'm in Los Angeles to work with previously incarcerated gang members, and Frank is one of them. The goal of this project is to support people who are integrating back into society (and into the workforce) and figure out what, exactly, makes for a successful reintegration. We are using a curric-ulum that I built from what little we already know—that people in this population are deeply traumatized but do not receive any mental health care over their lifespans, and if it is offered, they will often reject it because it is stigmatized. We also know that they are often identifiable by their tat-toos and so they face brutal daily discrimination, that there is very little by way of social support for these folks, and that over 83 percent of them will end up back in prison within three years.

At seventeen, Frank was sentenced to multiple life sen-tences for a triple homicide. He served nearly twenty years before being pardoned by California governor Jerry

Brown—who has taken on the task of rebalancing the scales of justice during his time in office.

You likely have bias about gang members. Honestly? It would be kind of weird if you didn't. They are almost always depicted in the news and Hollywood as wildly violent superpredators; serial killers with style who have chosen this violent and brutal life the way that some of us chose our majors in college. Nothing could be further from the truth. *Nobody* chooses to be in a gang. Children are born into them, jumped in before they hit double digits, join them as a last resort to protect their families and themselves. Also, the folks I was working with were former gang members. These are gang members that have left their gangs—a wildly dangerous move in most cases—and served their time. They deserve a second chance. And we all have more in common than you might think.

Frank has spent his entire adult life until now in prison. He's forty-three and at least twice my size. He's also seven with long, fluffy eyelashes like a cartoon cow and a smile that could effortlessly light up a small city during a blackout. And that seven-year-old is scared because he doesn't know how to read, but if he doesn't learn the words scrawled on the juvie bathroom walls fast enough, he won't be able to protect the smaller, prettier boys from the bigger, more predatory ones. This was his job. Perpetrate violence in order to protect people from worse violence. And, yeah, there are violences worse than death—the kind you survive.

As I'm wrapping up my session with Frank, it's approaching 10 a.m. and I find myself with my head in my hands, bracing against the sun and also the tears because Frank has just jubilantly asked if he could say a prayer with me—for me—before we get off the phone.

"I just want to pray with you, MC. Can we do that?"
"Of course, Frank."
"OK, but you have to close your eyes."
"Absolutely. Closed."

And then Frank says a prayer for peace for the both of us. Frank has no idea that my personal life is splitting at the seams. That every morning when I wake up, my first thought is, "This is a nightmare," and that every single night I find myself crying in the shower. He has no idea how badly I need peace, even a little, and I'm not even sure he knows how much he needs peace, but this moment where he says a prayer for my peace is one of those memories that gets crystalized like raw honey. It could stay just as alive, just as holy, if it were tucked away in an Egyptian tomb for five thousand years.

We end our call, and I can tell you exactly what Frank does with the rest of his day, because I know his entire routine. He likes to recite it to me at the beginning of every call because it's a way to exalt his freedom: the choices, his car, getting to pick what to listen to and drive whenever he feels like it, choosing what he eats. Frank finishes sweeping his room and goes to work. He listens to gospel music on his car stereo on the way home and stops at Five Guys. My day is also routine. I have more sessions with more guys just like Frank and not anything like Frank, and then I hide in the closet from the sun and cry.

What I don't see yet, and what Frank doesn't see either, is the joy thief that's standing right beside him while he sticks to his careful routine. This hypervigilance that saved Frank and the smaller, younger boys in prison is the very same hypervigilance that's poised to send him right back.

I see the joy thief one night when Frank calls me at 2 a.m. from jail. As a lifelong deep sleeper, I've learned to sleep light since I started working with these guys. If I don't answer by the third ring, they'll hang up. And when someone calls you from jail, you can't call back. I'm like a new mother, only instead of a newborn, I have forty former gang members waking me up in the middle of the night.

"Hello, this is a collect call from Ventura County Jail. Say yes if you would like to accept."
"*Fuck.* Yes! *Fuck!*"

Click. Click. And then Frank's voice comes on the line, and we are already in the middle of a conversation. No hello.

"MC, why are death and sex so tied together for me? Is that fucked up? Am I fucked up?"
"Because sex is the biggest 'fuck you' we can throw at death," I say. "That's not fucked up. It makes a lot of sense, actually. A genius rebellion. Is that why you called?"
"They killed Jimmy, MC. They killed him right on the street corner. I can still hear his mother screaming.

Screaming in the road. She was all folded over, MC, right there on the street. When they picked her up, she stayed folded over, like a shrimp or something. That's her last son, MC, you know? Her last one. But here's the thing, MC, my first thought was about Myra, though. That skirt she was wearing the other day. Hey, by the way, it wasn't my fault this time. They just took us all in. It wasn't my fault. Hey, MC, can we pray?"

"I know it's not your fault. It was never your fault, Frank. Do you know that? None of this has been your fault. It's just not that simple. And you're not fucked up. Yes, Frank, let's pray. Of course."

"OK, but you have to close your eyes."

"Absolutely."

How—and why—did Frank get sucked back in? How could he go from sweeping his room and praying with me and heading off to work to calling me from jail in just twelve hours? What happened, exactly, while I was crying in my closet? How did he so quickly join the 83 percent? Stories have layers, and there are far too many layers to this story to go into here. What I want to do instead is isolate the layer that you and I and Frank and all the rest of us have in common. It's the layer that explains why our hypervigilance gets us stuck in the dark and why we sometimes even choose to return to that dark even though it might be the opposite of what we want—or claim to want. It's also the layer that got Frank out of jail that night and a big part of what has kept him out ever since.

HYPERVIGILANCE AND THE
DEFAULT MODE NETWORK

Here's a humbling thing about being human: we think we have ourselves all figured out. We talk about ourselves as if it is possible to know ourselves completely. As if we don't have any blind spots. As if our motivations and our behaviors are always clear to us, and always aligned. The truth is that the project of being human is a project of stumbling, of discovering, and of becoming. *Sooooo* much of our psychology operates in the background, unconscious and preverbal. The upshot of this is that we don't always know ourselves or our motivations, and so sometimes our own behavior baffles us.

Our behavior can become baffling in many ways, but especially compelling to psychologists is the way that we hold vigil to negative thought loops and ruminations. Why is it that, when given the choice between meandering through any of a thousand positive memories, we lie in our beds at night stewing in the few negative ones? Why do we focus on that one critical piece of feedback when we got three times as many glowing reviews? Why do we pick apart our relationships because of tiny slights and failures instead of focusing on the many ways that our partners quietly show up for us? Why is it that so many people who get released from prison end up walking right back in?

As it turns out, a big part of the problem is in our neurobiology. Specifically, a network of brain regions that wire together to form the default mode network (DMN). Understanding the DMN can help us see how our worldview gets stamped with negativity, how this can force our hand, and how to change that.

When we talk about the brain, we can talk about several different things—the brain structures, blood flow between those structures, electrical activity and circuits, and brain chemistry. Each of these things is in a dynamic relationship with the others, but it can be helpful to isolate them and talk about them independently. Here we are going to mostly be talking about electrical activity and brain structures.

In the most basic terms possible, the DMN is a network of brain regions connected by neural circuits. These circuits fire up together when our mind is at rest and not engaged in a focused task, such as doing the laundry or making cookies. This network is thought to be responsible for any self-referential thinking, introspection, and mind wandering. Self-referential thoughts are when we connect information from the external world to the self. These can be positive—"The universe played this song on the radio at this moment just for me!"—or negative—"That group of girls across the courtyard is laughing, probably at me." Introspection occurs any time we contemplate our own conscious thoughts and feelings—"That conversation with my sister really bummed me out, and I'm having a hard time shaking the sadness." And mind wandering happens any time our mind takes a detour—you might find yourself fantasizing about a trip to Italy while making dinner or remembering that time you took a road trip to the beach with your friends in high school. Because the DMN is a network that spools up most prominently when we are at rest, it is sometimes referred to as the "baseline" or "resting state" of the brain.

The DMN wasn't discovered until the late 1990s, and, like many world-changing discoveries, it was found by a total fluke. When researchers performed brain-imaging studies in the 1950s using PET and MRI technology, they noticed that the brains of their participants were active even when they were not completing a task. Assuming that the brain activity that happened during rest was just "noise," they always selected it out of their data. For fifty years, that noise went unexamined. That is, until a group of researchers started wondering whether there might be a signal in the noise. They discovered that a consistent pattern of activity was present across participants, and so they started mapping out this network and theorizing about its purpose. As it turns out, the noise wasn't noise at all—it was a foundational part of what makes each of us a self.

I always think of the DMN like a TV that is always on the same channel and running in the background of the living room. If you're talking on the phone to someone, or cooking dinner, or working on something that requires a lot of focus, you're not going to pay much attention to that TV. But as soon as you hang up, finish cooking dinner, and file your last TPS report, the TV starts to become much more noticeable. It's almost like it physically gets louder even if you didn't turn up the volume. Just because it's running in the background does not mean it is unimportant—the DMN forms the foundation of your sense of self and your worldview.

The DMN is made up of five brain structures. Think of

these brain structures as a group of your best buddies in high school. The medial prefrontal cortex (mPFC) is your brainy friend that has a part-time job at the reference desk in the library. She is in charge of self-referential thinking, introspection, and sorting out information as it relates to yourself, your thoughts, and your emotions. She's the first one to notice when you're not feeling like yourself and asks you about it—and has two or three ideas about why. She is who you go to when you need to think through a decision or get a reality check on an emotional response you are having that you can't quite understand. The mPFC is a good friend to have.

The posterior cingulate cortex (PCC) is your romantic, dreamy friend who sits in the back of the classroom doodling her girlfriend's name on her notebooks. PCC is in charge of memory retrieval ("Remember when she made you that play-list? Swoon!"), self-reflection ("You're such an evolved person now that you're in a real, adult relationship!"), and daydreaming ("Maybe we can convert an old VW bus and drive across the country together!"). To do all this, she pulls together information from various brain regions and integrates it. You go to her when you need to figure out how different pieces of a story fit together, and when you have forgotten how to dream. PCC can be kind of annoying at times, but she's necessary.

The precuneus is the artist and dancer in the group. He's elegant and coordinated. He's great at coming up with visual imagery, processing things with you, and retrieving memories. He remembers that your colors are winter, and that you hate high-waisted jeans, and that your last boyfriend told you you couldn't pull off orange. When you hang out, he helps you rearrange your bedroom and teaches you how to dance. (Precuneus is a weird name, but he owns it—claims it's Greek or something.)

The lateral temporal cortex (LTC) is the writer, so he's quick to process and render experiences into language and observes social relationships keenly. He listens to everything and never forgets a face. He plays a major role in how we understand and relate to others, and when you need to talk through a confusing encounter, he is your go-to. "OK, so she didn't answer the text right away, that's true—but she's never been a good texter. Also, have you ever noticed how freaked out she looks when she gets a phone notification? I think she's just better one-on-one and in person." LTC can save you from your own worst instincts sometimes.

Last but not at all least, the hippocampus is the historian of the group. She's the friend that remembers everything. She's stored away memories from when you were five and can pull them out at a moment's notice to remind you in case you need it. "No, no, no," she might say, "you had those round tortoiseshell frames in first grade. Absolute disaster. Let's go with navy in a more rectangular shape." She's the one you go to when you are trying to remember that seventh-grade English teacher who was just so weird, or whether that argument with your mother about joining the Girl Scouts really happened or if you saw it in a movie. Hippocampus is your human hard drive.

Each of these friends has a distinct personality, but together they form a complete and coherent worldview.

They have grown up in the same place, have similar experiences, and share opinions and values. If you were faced with a relationship conundrum and asked them for advice at lunch, you'd likely get a very unified set of answers—albeit from different perspectives. And just like a group of teenage friends, the DMN can be *influenced*.

As your ride-or-die friends, the job they take most seriously is protecting you. This is why they are so easily swayed by negative experiences. They're always well-intentioned, but they can sometimes err on the side of being just a tad overprotective. You might forget all the bad stuff that Jason did while you were dating because "C'mon, have you seen his eyes?!," but they will remind you—quickly, sternly, and unequivocally—so that you avoid the mistake of getting into that bad relationship again. This can quickly get difficult to navigate. It can start to feel like they don't trust you to make your own decisions, like you have to stop taking risks altogether to appease them.

This is your DMN. Wired together, these structures in the brain are constantly telling you who you are, where you are, what the world is like, and how you should move about in it. Though it may mostly run in the background, that does not mean its influence is minor.

So, why so negative, DMN?!

From an evolutionary standpoint, the brain is wired to seek safety and predictability—so it automatically imprints negative experiences and situations, because this puts us at a survival advantage. The more you remember what might be dangerous, the more likely you are to avoid it. But if all you are doing is remembering what might be dangerous, you can end up missing out on this moment and what's good about it.

Many of the key areas involved in the DMN are related to memory. They are keeping track and filing away negative experiences, and as you move through life, the negative can start to stack up like empties after spring break. Remember how self-referential thoughts can be positive—"The universe played this song on the radio at this moment just for me!"—or negative—"That group of girls across the courtyard is laughing, probably at me"? If you have had a lot of negative experiences, your mind can start automatically defaulting to negative thoughts and worries. The whole world starts to look and feel negative. All your background thoughts get consumed by worry and flashes of the bad things that have happened to you. This tendency creates negative feedback loops, where we get stuck in repetitive, ruminating, and unproductive patterns of thinking. These loops can strangle hope and joy—but only if you let them.

Remember the TV analogy from earlier? If that TV was stuck on and at the loudest volume, you'd have a really hard time doing any of the other things that you needed to do— make dinner, talk on the phone, do your work. That's what it's like when you have a lot of negativity racing around in your DMN. It's loud and trying to get your attention to remind you that the world is dangerous, and so it becomes impossible to focus on anything else. Like hope. And joy.

Did you know the word *negative* comes from the root *negate*, meaning "to deny"? When your DMN is stuck in a pattern of ruthless rumination, going over every mistake you've ever made and worst-casing every single scenario, it is denying you your right to hope and joy. It is sentencing you to multiple life sentences inside your mind. Here's the good news: the DMN can be reset. So, when it is running a negative and scary script and getting in the way of us connecting to joy, we can pardon ourselves. All we need to do is learn how to activate a different mode to shake up the focus. This requires intention and a bit of a commitment—but it's not nearly as hard as you'd think.

Frank gets out of jail quickly. He had done nothing wrong; the police had arrested almost anyone present in order to get some control over the situation. The next session that we have is in person. We meet at a Starbucks and sit outside in uncomfortable steel chairs.

"I went out to my car today, MC, and there were four crows on the hood. Four, MC. Do you know what that means?"
"Wait, I think I actually do . . . one is for sorrow, two is for mirth, three for a wedding, four for . . . is it death?"
Frank nods slowly, his head bent down, both hands wrapped around his cup as if it were winter in New England. We are sitting underneath a huge palm tree, and in the shade it's still probably ninety-two degrees.
"Death, MC. It's following me. It's everywhere out here. When I was in, all I wanted was to get out. Feel the sunshine. Go to the beach. Sit at a restaurant. Drive my car. When they came in that day and told me it was time to go, I didn't even get my stuff, MC. I was afraid that if I took any time—if I even turned around—they would change their

minds. But it's following me still. Death is following me. I feel like it's following me. It always will." He shivers.

Frank's DMN has been influenced by so much darkness. His DMN isn't a group of high school friends; it's a gang. The members jumped him in at seven and got him to believe that the world was inherently violent, dangerous, dark. So, at seven he started believing that being more violent, more dangerous, and more dark was the only way to survive. Hypervigilance was the only way forward, the only safety on offer. So, this joy thief became the boss of the DMN gang and dictated how Frank lived for forty-three years—attentive, cautious, and braced for the next terrible thing. That is, until he got out of prison, and all the goodness and freedom on the outside tricked him into letting his guard down. Into sleeping well and enjoying breakfast sandwiches. And his DMN can't possibly have that; it's far too dangerous. So, it's trying to protect him by denying him access to everything good that he found in the world.

Frank does need protection—but not from the world; from this gang inside his head led by hypervigilance. He needs protection from his own DMN, and in that moment, I must admit, I had no fucking clue how to do that. Frank was already doing all the right things. Since he'd been out, he'd been fighting back with gratitude, prayers, his broom, and Egg McMuffins. He was working and going to meetings. He wasn't going back in. But, since Jimmy was killed, Frank's DMN has been trying to tell him it's not enough. Both he and I could feel the pull. This is a precarious situation. We've got to reset Frank's

DMN away from this hypervigilance, and *fast*, or that 83 percent will come for him.

> "Let's walk on the beach," I say. "It's going to be a crazy beautiful sunset." Frank looks up, and for a millisecond the light is back in his eyes.
> "OK, MC, I see what you're doing, OK." Then back to dark again. I'll take it. I can work with a millisecond.

The Manhattan Beach boardwalk is three blocks away, and so we walk down—passing rows of multimillion-dollar glass houses. We make an odd pair, Frank and I. He's over a foot taller than me, and has more tattoos than I have years to my life. We walk along the boardwalk and stop in front of a mile-high beachfront house that has bright-blue-tinted floor-to-ceiling windows and life-size Disney-character sculptures on each of the three balconies. It's a bit like an abandoned shopping mall from the '90s. We stop and marvel for a minute and then both start laughing. In no time, Frank is doubled over with tears streaming down his face. "Rich people, MC! Rich. People! *EmmmCeeee!*"

I'm so grateful for the moment—the levity, the laughter, the shift, the trust—that I'm in tears too. When we stop laugh-crying and start walking again, I take the leap.

> "I know that you feel like death is following you. For what it's worth, I feel like it's following you, too. It scares me. But just because it's following you doesn't mean it's the only thing. This is all here too. It's all in the same day. In

the same hour, sometimes in the same minute. We notice the bad because it makes such a scene in its chasing—you know? But the good? The good doesn't chase, it sits. It's quieter, doesn't fight for your attention. So, we have to pay attention to it. When we only look at what's chasing us, we miss so much . . ."

"They got Jimmy."

"I know."

"His mother . . ."

He trails off and then stops at a bench shaped like a seashell and sits down, looking straight into the sea. We sit there for a few minutes and watch people walking along the sand, playing volleyball and drinking beer, sitting and reading their magazines in the sun. We're both thinking about Jimmy's mother, folded into the concrete, screaming. Frank looks at me after a few minutes, and the light is back in his face.

"MC, do you know why birds sing in the morning?" Feels like a bit of a non sequitur, but we're both lost at the moment, so why not?

"You know, I have never thought about that in my entire life. I have no idea why."

"They sing to let each other know that they made it through the night."

I stare at Frank. I'm so stunned by the beauty of that fact—and of learning that fact in this moment and in this way—that I don't say anything at all.

"Isn't that beautiful? As soon as they wake up—chirp,
chirp, chirp—hey, guys, I'm still here! Who else? Anyone
want a breakfast sandwich?" We laugh.
"How—on earth—do you know that?"
"Oh, I used to raise doves in the yard."
"Doves?"
"Yeah. You know, mourning doves? They're real sweet.
Loyal too."

Something about the image of this tiny bird in Frank's
giant mitt refocuses the whole project. The positives and the
negatives of this hypervigilance—the kind of attention that
keeps baby birds alive and the kind that is tricking Frank
into believing that the darkness is all there is. Yes, we need
to reset Frank's DMN. With something other than Myra's
skirt this time. And this feels like a huge job—an overhaul of
such proportions that it will require precisely what we do not
have—but maybe that's a trick too. After all, just because
humans can measure things does not mean that we understand the scale of things. Maybe this is a huge job that will
require tiny steps instead of big ones. Tiny steps repeated
over and over and over and over again—more ninja sneaking
up on her victim than battalion marching into town. One
whose answer is so obvious and small it will seem ridiculous.

This is often how we grow—bit by tiny bit, step by pains-
taking step. We miss this because the stories that we like to
tell about growth are so much grander. We brush over the
stories of the bleeding and the sweating and focus instead on

the descriptions of the pinnacles and peaks that we finally reach. But that's not the whole story. In fact, it's usually a really small piece of the story. The real journey belongs instead to the tininess. The decision that you made to get stronger. Every day that you went to the gym and ran, or cycled, or climbed, or lifted—most days exactly the same, some days a little bit less, and some days a little bit more. And remember the stalactites and stalagmites?

The work of rewiring the brain is not always exciting. But it is possible. And that's exciting.

"Here's what we're going to do, Frank. We're going to flip the script."

"Rebellion, MC! I love it! That's crack-a-lackin'!"

"Listen, maybe the darkness is chasing us. And we can't really do anything about it—it's just going to happen. The deaths are going to keep coming whether we want them to or not. But also? Fuck that! We're not going to borrow any grief from tomorrow. Instead, we're going to turn around and chase the light. And we're going to gather all the light we possibly can. Every single day. And we're going to capture it like lightning bugs in a jar. Keep it on the bedside table. And eventually we'll have so much of it that the darkness will decide it had better chase someone else. Because, yeah, there are crows on the car, but there are also doves in the yard. Doves that you raised. The doves are there too, and they just don't do creepy crow shit."

Frank is laughing. "Oh, I'm so in, MC."

Here is one of the tools that Frank and I came up with. I can't say that this is the thing that kept him at his job and out of prison, but I can say that it did help shake up his DMN and shift his worldview away from negativity and rumination. And that this left him with a much stronger foundation. The work of laying a new foundation might not be as sexy as decorating your entire downstairs and putting it on Pinterest, but, without it, you have nowhere to live at all.

~~MINDFULNESS~~ REVERENCE FOR THE MOMENTS WHEN DEATH IS CHASING YOU

When I first drafted this chapter, I included a simple mindfulness exercise. But here's the thing: you probably already know about mindfulness. You've heard it from Ram Dass and Thich Nhat Hanh and Oprah and every marketing-chick-turned-yogi on your Instagram feed. Most everything you've read about it is probably true. Mindfulness is an incredibly powerful tool that you can fold into your everyday life as simply as you fold blueberries into scone batter. Making dishwashing a mindfulness moment has changed my whole evening routine. But to shake up the DMN, we need something different. Especially when the crows are gathering on the hoods of our cars reminding us that death is chasing us.

Enter Reverence.

Working with these guys for the two years that I did was an experience that left me wordless for almost five. Even now it feels impossible to communicate. It was like being set on fire. I had been a coach for seven years, and most of my work felt like it was happening in some kind of trenches; I had been working with first responders and veterans and victims of brutal abuse, and none of them had been taught anything helpful about trauma. But these trenches were different. Not because there is a hierarchy of trauma that made healing more difficult. But because none of my previous clients were facing such dire statistics about their futures on top of the healing they were doing. That 83 percent woke me up at 3:47 a.m. Curled around my pillow like a viper, hissing in my ear.

According to some metrics, I know that the work we were doing helped. We had only two guys out of forty recidivate in the two years we were working with them. We helped them get employed and housed and stay that way. It didn't just take a village; it took a small army. We worked with social services organizations, employers, and advocates. So, I think it's fair to assume that we had some positive impact. But every single day I worked with them, I felt like the scales were tipped far in the wrong direction—I was getting so much more from them than I could ever give.

Each one of these guys came crashing into my life and rebuilt a little piece of my cracked foundation. In place of grief and doubt and pain, they poured in holiness and reverence and faith. In each conversation, while I flailed around trying to help, they effortlessly smoothed and leveled the concrete, making sure it dried without any air bubbles. And I hadn't even told them it was cracked. They just knew.

I think I had such a hard time writing about this work because it flattened me with reverence. It left me stunned and speechless and in a kind of love that I will never recover from. It felt like the first time I really saw stars in New Mexico after living in the crowded Northeast for all my twenty-four years. Or when I walked into the ICU room where my father had suffered a fatal stroke and saw that when we die, we *actually leave* our bodies. Or when I looked out at the mountainous horizon in Colorado and thought for a second that it must be some kind of fake backdrop. Reverence like that sets you back on your heels, stops you from breathing, steals your every thought.

And do you know what else reverence does? It hits a hard reset button on your DMN.

Reverence—or awe—returns us to our default settings—before the worry and negativity flooded our synapses. No one really knows exactly why yet. But we do know that when research participants engage in something that causes this feeling, it turns the volume on the DMN channel all the way down.[1] When it gets turned down, the DMN effectively resets itself, and when it comes back online, the connections are less stifled than before. This openness in the channel allows us to establish new connections and shake out some of the negativity.

I didn't teach Frank anything; I just reminded him of what he already knew. Of what *he* had taught *me*. And then turned it into homework. I asked him to absolutely drench himself in that reverence, that awe, as often as he possibly could, every single day—and to report back.

Frank—no surprise here—does *not* fuck around, and he took this more seriously than I ever could have hoped. He went camping to get a real look at the stars outside of LA ("I always thought that was just a white-person hobby!"), he set his alarm and drove out to the beach at sunrise and then back for sunset just to see which one was better ("Sunrise, MC, but what a date idea to take a special lady at sunset, you feel me?"), a football game at LMU with his cousins ("All those people yelling the same cheer at the same time!"), Griffith Observatory at night ("LA is so beautiful all lit up like that. Even the dirty parts."), and the Broad Museum ("The Basquiat stopped me in my tracks. I couldn't even move."). In a matter of weeks, it felt like the crows were gone. Frank was brighter, restored. I could feel his resilience strengthening. He worried less and now so did I. Likely the crows were still there, hovering unsettlingly. But we weren't paying attention to them anymore, and that changed the whole damn thing.

Because Frank was so open and willing, he quickly found what some of us resist, which is that awe is literally all around us all the time. We just have to tune into it. In fact, the research supports what Frank already knows: there are at least eight sources of awe that we can encounter in our everyday lives. No need to go trip balls on ayahuasca to find it (please don't do that). The eight sources that have been identified are the moral beauty of others, which is what we feel when we witness someone doing something good; collective movement, like when you dance in the kitchen with your kids or go to a yoga class; nature, which you can encounter by simply opening your window; visual design; music; spirituality; big ideas; and encountering the beginning and end of life.[2] Awe is everywhere. And it beats back hypervigilance.

So, this is the tool I'm giving to you: find sights or experiences or art that makes you feel that slack-jawed reverence and lean all the way into it. Watch your DMN reset. First, we have to figure out what gives you that feeling.

FIGHTING HYPERVIGILANCE WITH AWE

Step 1) Find a quiet space. Sit comfortably and close your eyes. Reflect on what awe and reverence mean to you. What do these words bring up? How do they feel in your mouth? What memories start to pop up when you think about them? If the concepts feel too big, try and scale down. When I think about awe, I immediately remember the handful of times that I was stunned by nature—standing on a mountaintop in Colorado, seeing a sky completely full of stars in the desert in California. If I scale down, I remember the documentary series I just watched about African penguins (a.k.a. the jackass penguin—no, I'm not joking). When I think about reverence, I am reminded of ancient churches I visited in Italy, and old cemeteries in Massachusetts. When I scale that concept down, I remember how that new Billie Eilish song actually took my breath away the first time I heard it, and how a conversation with my friend Chris about the afterlife made me marvel at the fact that we get to be alive during the same timeline. Wherever you find your mind wandering around these concepts, make a commitment to be open to experiences of awe and reverence in the coming days. (And, no, you don't need fourteen-thousand-foot mountains!)

Step 2) For an entire week, actively seek out experiences or places that might inspire awe or reverence. This could look like taking deep breaths while you do the dishes and letting the warm water pour over your hands, taking long walks in the woods, watching the fog roll in over a landscape, really listening to that song blasting into your headphones, sitting in silent places of worship, going to museums and losing yourself in works of art, taking a slightly different route home than you usually do, making something for dinner that takes a long time but that you really love, or watching documentaries about bower birds. Anything.

Step 3) Whenever you find yourself in a potentially awe-inspiring situation, pause. Put your phone down. Take deep breaths. Observe your surroundings— like, really observe them. Pay attention to how your body feels. Do you feel grounded? Energized? Does that wonder make you feel small? Huge? If this part feels scary or weird, you are not alone. We live in a culture right now that does not value taking a pause, let alone checking in with our bodies. Start with one or more of these prompts:

What details in my surroundings have I never noticed before?

How does the light change the scene?

What sounds can I hear if I really listen?

How does my body respond to these sensations?

Step 4) Write it. After the experience, write what it was at the top of the page and then let yourself free write about it. As in, "Night sky," and then free associate. Don't worry about whether you are making sense or whether someone else would understand what you wrote—don't even worry about whether you are writing sentences. Just write. At the end of the week, review your journal entries. Looking back now, what surprised you? Can you see any changes in how you are thinking or feeling?

You'll be happy to know that Frank beat the odds. It has been more than four years now since he has been out, and he has stayed out. Most of the guys that we worked with stayed out. It's not easy, but many of them are holding down multiple jobs, helping other guys who are coming out of prison, buying breakfast sandwiches for whoever needs them.

Homeboy Industries—one of the organizations we worked with—is a nonprofit that provides hope, training, and support to previously incarcerated gang members. Anyone who walks through their doors is welcomed with open arms and supported in whatever way they need. Run by Jesuit priest Father Greg Boyle, the place is full of awe, full of reverence, full of holiness. One of the daily rituals that keeps the place grounded and tuned in is called the thought for the day. At 9:00 a.m. on the dot, a bell rings, everyone gathers in the main hall, and a microphone gets handed to someone who speaks about anything that is on their mind. Anything.

On April 28, 2021, Homeboy opened back up after being closed for the pandemic for a year. At 9:00 a.m., the bell rang, and Father Greg handed the microphone to a former gang member named Robert. Robert came to Homeboy when he got out and has been working in and with it for fourteen years. He talked about awe and how it transforms us—if we let it. He says it far better than I ever could, so I'm going to hand the microphone to him:

"Good morning. All right, I guess I'm back up on opening day. You know what, it's ironic—because you know when we had to close down because of the pandemic, I actually prayed us out, and I remember saying that this too will pass, you know. So, it's an honor for me to do the thought of the day during opening day.

"You know I took the train today, and I was tripping out, I was listening to this preacher, right, and he said, 'Behold, stand in awe, and be amazed.' . . . It's about opening your heart and opening your heart to the process. You know there's many steps in this process, but once you surrender to this process—I ask that you guys do the same, you know that you should be open, that you embrace this place of grace and allow it to shape you. . . . You'll see the beauty that this place does to every one of us, you know? So, behold, stand in awe, and be amazed."[3]

You heard him. Behold. Stand in awe and be amazed.

CHAPTER 3

Emotional Numbing: Making Meaning in the Meaninglessness

Romance and poetry, ivy, lichens and wallflowers need ruin to make them grow.

—Nathaniel Hawthorne

RICHIE'S THERAPIST JUST DOESN'T GET IT. AT LEAST THAT'S what Richie tells me in our first session. He found me online and he says he doesn't really have any trauma, but he just feels like I might be able to get it. He's hit a therapeutic plateau, and everything feels a little, well, flat. Richie is doing fine, but there's just something, like, missing? And so, we begin.

Richie is twenty-three and so goddamn endearing it's hard

not to grin sometimes while he's talking. He's earnest and accidentally hilarious and I sort of wish I could adopt him, but that would probably be inappropriate. Richie's life is not atypical. He grew up in a nice suburban town to parents who wanted him. His dad was a casting director, so Richie spent just about every millisecond of free time starting from the day he was born watching or talking about movies. He was an active and happy kid, but things started to shift almost imperceptibly when his parents split. Richie was ten and the world started to get a little dark in ways he couldn't really describe. You can actually see the light in his eyes start to go out in his childhood photos, which I had him bring in when he mentioned that he struggled to figure out why these happy memories were making him so sad.

The problem was that Richie was a kid with big feelings, and there was no one there to feel them with him. So, he swept them under the rug, adapted, and moved forward, through high school, college, and into his first dream job. The dream job that both he and his dad had wanted for him since he was six. Here's the thing about stepping directly into your dreams—there is almost always a disorienting distance between the dream you had in your head your whole life and the reality of that dream. Richie was disappointed and couldn't figure out why. He was stretched thin and stressed out and then his girlfriend dumped him. Following the dream trope, she had been the girl of his dreams, and he was blindsided by the breakup. And then it was like all the darkness that no one had helped him navigate since he was ten, all the confusing feelings that he had swept under the rug came pouring out all at once, and life seemed completely unlivable. So, Richie tried to kill himself. Three times.

All attempts were unsuccessful, but three is a pattern, and suddenly Richie and everyone in his life had to come to grips with the fact that he was *really* struggling with mental illness and had been for a long time. We don't treat mental and physical illnesses the same in our culture. For the most part, we allow for physical illnesses and ailments. Sometimes we even make them virtuous—we call cancer survivors brave and refer to their illnesses as battles. But suicide is too dark for our culture to look at, much less talk about. We tell ourselves that we have a hard time talking about it because it's so rare that we couldn't possibly know what to say, but that's a crock of shit. We have a hard time talking about it because it's so terrifyingly universal that the only way to hem it in is to make it taboo. This is deeply, life-threateningly misguided. No idea is as dangerous as one that has been made taboo.

I get where Richie is coming from—sort of. At least, I get the part about how the world can suddenly seem entirely unlivable. About six months after my father suddenly died (don't worry, virtuous cancer), I became gripped with *relentless* panic attacks. They would hit at random, and they were so intense and visceral I would often actually hit the floor, grasping for any ground. I became so incredibly uncomfortable that I started to fear for my own life. Not because I *wanted* to die, but because I became convinced that I would kill myself just to make it stop. The thing that made this so much worse—and, frankly, put me in much more danger—was the fact that talking about it seemed more impossible than going through with it.

Before we get further into Richie's story, I need you to know something. Anyone who attempts suicide does so because they believe down to their very toes that there is *no other choice*. No possible way to continue. Part of the devastation of losing someone to suicide is that you might believe down to *your* very toes that there *were* many other choices. Those who survive suicide attempts are still left to grapple with some of that same devastation. You are left answering for yourself and for those who did die by suicide. And everyone has the same question: *Why?* We think that if we can understand the *why* behind suicide, we could stop it. If we could just get our heads around some strong and justifiable reason, it wouldn't be so scary. But here's the truth: there is no strong and justifiable why—not a satisfying one, at least.

Richie is still looking for his own reasons, and even to him, none of them feel satisfying. This is the plateau; this is what is keeping him stuck. Why did he try to end his life, and three times? What could have possibly been bad enough to bring him to that point, and how can he *possibly* trust that the next bad day isn't going to be the thing that sends him over the edge?

"It was my dream job. Which is kind of what made it scary. It was way more responsibility than I was ready for, but I think if I had just taken a break maybe I could have gone back. . . . And Kelsey? I mean, she was so far out of my league I honestly could never figure out what she was doing

**with me anyway. And my doubts about that made me act
pretty shitty to her. It shouldn't have been that surprising
that she ended it."**

Richie isn't suicidal anymore. But that doesn't mean he's
OK. He feels stuck and flat. Every time it feels like the nose
of the plane is about to go up, it comes back down again.
We keep going over successes and signs of life. Objectively,
Richie is doing really well. He's got a solid routine, he has a
great group of friends, he's got a new career, and not only
can he totally handle it, but he also keeps getting promoted.
He's got a new girlfriend. When great things happen to him,
though, they don't *feel* great to him. Once, he told me at the
very beginning of a session that he had gotten the second big
promotion in a year at the job he didn't think he was going
to land.

**"Promoted! Again! Richie, that's huge!" I'm practically
shouting as he tells me this, shooting my hands up in the air
in celebration.
"Yeah," he says, his affect flat. "I guess it's pretty rare or
whatever."**

It's one hundred times easier for me to celebrate for Richie
than it is for Richie to celebrate for Richie. None of his wins
are landing. Nothing feels meaningful. In fact, it all feels
numb, and Richie is afraid that if we don't figure out why,
he's going to end up right back where he started—flooded
in the dark with a bottle of pills in his hand. And Richie's

afraid of the dark. The thing that no one tells you about being afraid of the dark is that if you don't face that fear, you end up afraid of the light too.

Our impulse when we are afraid of something is to turn away from it. To turn to anything else. To turn it down. Sometimes the only way to cope with this fear is to numb. We numb with distraction, with drama, with alcohol and Xanax and our own exhaustion. Like all our other adaptations, there is some genius here. We can't bear to feel, and so we find whatever we can that will turn down the volume on those feelings. This is emotional numbing, and it is the joy thief that's moved into Richie's apartment like that friend with questionable hygiene who asked to crash on the couch for a few weeks and keeps promising to head out looking for jobs tomorrow. It is a protective mechanism our brains employ to shield us from whatever is overwhelming. It's completely natural, and much of the time it's lifesaving, allowing us to function when our emotions become too much to bear. But there's a significant downside to this coping strategy when it persists for too long: it doesn't discriminate between the emotions it blunts. When we numb ourselves to avoid the darkness, we also close ourselves off from the light.

The human brain just isn't designed to selectively mute only the negative emotions. When we suppress our sadness, fear, or anger, we also dampen our capacity for joy, love, and excitement. This is why people like Richie, who have experienced profound emotional pain, often describe feeling "flat" or "numb" even when their external circumstances seem to be turning positive. It's not that Richie can't see the good things in his life—it's that he can't *feel* them. The very mechanisms that protected him from despair are now keeping him from happiness.

This numbing is what created the plateau—it swept in and leveled any possible highs. It's why Richie's wins don't feel like wins and why nothing feels meaningful, despite the objective successes in his life. The emotional guardrails he has subconsciously erected to keep the darkness at bay are also keeping him from fully engaging with life. And this is a common experience for people who have been through significant emotional trauma or stress. They become adept at shutting down their feelings to survive, but in the process, they lose touch with the full spectrum of human experience.

The tragedy of emotional numbing is that it is a kind of emotional suicide. We turn to it only when it feels like the only option. When the pain is too great, numbing seems like a small price to pay for peace. But over time, the cost becomes much too high. Life becomes muted, and the ability to connect with others, to find joy, and to feel alive slips further out of reach. This is the paradox of emotional numbing: it's a solution that creates its own set of problems, and it can be difficult to reverse. Difficult, but not impossible.

"Richie, this is going to sound really strange, but I need to send you an essay by a French existentialist, and I need you to read it. We can talk about it next time we meet. It's called 'The Myth of Sisyphus' by Albert Camus."

Richie laughs while he takes a note. "Got it. The myth of what?"

"Sisyphus. Just trust me. And I've heard all the jokes, OK?"

We need existentialism to get us out of this mess, because it's going to do two things: one, help Richie learn how to see in the dark, and two, understand how the depths he went to made him a lot deeper too. We just need to take a really swift detour into existentialism.

THE EXISTENTIALISTS AND THE ABYSS

If you do an image search for Albert Camus, you will find him immortalized in a well-tailored suit under a wool trench coat with the collar popped, staring with a half-smirk into the middle distance, dark, wavy hair slicked back and a cigarette hanging out of the left side of his mouth. He looks like very elegant trouble.

I won't bore you with the details of Camus's life that brought him to birth a whole philosophical movement dedicated to finding light in the darkness. All you need to know is that he was a dude who got *very* familiar with the dark. As he explored those dark caverns, two crystal-clear formations caught his eye—absurdity and meaninglessness—gleaming like rare gems hidden deep within. He and his existentialist friends polished them into guiding tenets, treasures pulled from the depths. The first will sound like a Zen koan: existence precedes essence. This just means that we do not arrive in the world with a preset destiny. We are not objects; we are beings, which means that we must live, and choose, and make mistakes, and fail, and succeed in order to create our essence. We exist first; our essence is created as we live. By us.

If the first tenet sounds like a koan, the second will sound like the battle cry of a rebellious sixteen-year-old: life has no meaning. In fact, life is absurd. Wherever you look for some preordained meaning, you will find ridiculousness instead. This second idea tends to split groups cleanly in two. People either grab hold of this idea of meaninglessness and drape it over themselves as if the idea is as appealing to inhabit as Camus's trench coat, or they say, "tsk, tsk," and turn away in judgment of what they believe to be an immature and potentially dangerous ideology. Both decisions are made in haste and therefore miss the critical clause that immediately follows from "life has absolutely no inherent meaning," which is, *"except for the meaning we give it."*

There is no such thing as destiny; there are no preset meanings for you to go search for. There is no meaning here at all. Our lives are meaningful *not* because we are predestined; they are meaningful because *we make them so.* The upshot of being born without any preset essence and into a world without meaning is that we all have ultimate and complete authority over our lives. This also means there is no external authority that can a) tell you what you should do, or b) judge you. There is one thing and one thing only that you can do wrong in the eyes of the existentialists, and that is to fail to take that radical responsibility over your life. Life is a blank canvas, and we have complete and total responsibility over what goes on it. Grab your paintbrushes, say the existentialists; we've got work to do.

What does suicide have to do with any of this? Suicide is relevant to existentialism because the ultimate proof of our radical freedom is that we can choose our own death at any time. For the existentialists—and you don't have to buy this, but just try and comprehend it before you reject it—the fact that we can choose our own death is the ultimate sign of our freedom.

This might sound completely counterintuitive, but go with me for a second. There is a way in which the thought of suicide can be an adaptation. In moments of deep despair or entrapment, the thought of suicide can paradoxically feel like a lifeline—an option, a last resort that seems to promise relief from an unbearable situation. For someone who feels completely trapped, just knowing there's an ultimate escape can provide a sense of control and autonomy in an otherwise helpless moment. It's important to understand that this thought can actually be a kind of adaptive response, an attempt by the mind to create a safety net in the face of overwhelming circumstances. Recognizing that the thought of suicide is an attempt at adaptation can make the thought feel less frightening and more understandable, revealing it as a signal of how urgently we need to create room to breathe, to find other ways of reclaiming freedom, or to make choices that help us feel less cornered. It reminds us that we're wired to seek out a way forward, even if that forward path sometimes first appears in darkness.

Let me tell you the story of Camus's absurd hero Sisyphus (briefly, I promise) and why I sent it to Richie. You may not know Sisyphus by name, but you have definitely seen his likeness. He is the muscle-bound, shirtless man from Greek mythology who is depicted in sculpture and on motivational posters rolling an enormous boulder up a steep hill (not to be confused with the muscle-bound, shirtless man holding the world above his head—that's Atlas). Sisyphus has been condemned to roll a boulder up a hill. This may not sound so bad, but as soon as he gets to the top of the hill, the boulder rolls right back down, and Sisyphus has to go get it. Again, and again, and again, and—you guessed it, again. For eternity.

Camus was obsessed with Sisyphus because while the vast majority of Sisyphus's existence is determined, there's a critical catch: even the all-powerful Greek gods couldn't make him completely determined. They had to give him enough lucidity and enough freedom for him to experience his own torture and know it as torture. That freedom means that Sisyphus gets to choose *how* he completes his infinite task. He can do it full of scorn; he can do it laughing. He can taunt the gods each and every time, chanting, "Yes, you took away most of my freedom, but you couldn't take it all. You can't catch me; nobody can!" In this way, Sisyphus is infinitely doomed *and* simultaneously infinitely free. Just like us. Wait, what?

We may not be condemned to roll boulders up hills, but if we're being honest, life feels Sisyphean sometimes. OK. A lot of the time. There are lots and *lots* of things that are determined for us—things we do not choose and cannot control. What Sisyphus reminds us of is that we are not and cannot ever be completely determined. And unlike him, we are free in two ways: first, we can choose the way we complete our determined tasks. You can wake up tomorrow morning and bemoan your alarm, slog through your day, complain through dinner, doom scroll for a couple of hours, and then go to bed. Or you can jump out of bed excited for your first sip of coffee, listen to your favorite dance music in the shower, laugh with your coworkers about memes during work, and go out to dinner with friends. We have an additional freedom, which is the choice whether to go on at all. Unlike Sisyphus—who is in hell and will remain there, well, forever—we are not. The fact that we all have the choice to live or not live each and every moment is the thing that sets us free. This is why Camus begins his very famous essay "The Myth of Sisyphus" with "There is but one truly serious philosophical problem, and that is suicide."[1] That's one hell of an opening line, Al.

I want to make this really very clear: suicide is *not* what the existentialists would recommend. To them, suicide is just proof that we're really, unmistakably, and completely free. That doesn't mean they think we should do it. To end your life is to end the freedom to create your life—and that's the only currency we've got. What most people get wrong about existentialism is this idea that life is absurd and meaningless is not the end of the story, it's the *beginning*. It's not suicide we should aim at; it's embracing the freedom that we are given and building ourselves a world right on top of the abyss.

One of the purposes of existentialism is to help us understand that we are (terrifyingly) free and have radical responsibility over our lives. Another purpose, though, is to help us cope when we find ourselves facing the abyss. After all, Camus was facing the abyss when he wrote it. I think part of the reason he wrote was to leave dispatches from the darkness—literary roadmaps that other people might find when they got plummeted into it. We all have a moment when we encounter the abyss for the first time. Richie had faced the abyss head-on, and he was carrying his terror with him. I plummeted into it when my father died.

Since the abyss is, well, an abyss, it can be a little hard to describe. Have you ever lived in a place that has wall-to-wall carpeting? If so, you will know that at some point, your curiosity takes over and you peel a piece of that carpeting back to see what's underneath. Encountering the abyss is just like this, except that when you peel back the wall-to-wall carpet of existence, you don't find the original fir planks. Instead, there is a dark, swirling nothingness. It's horrifying and captivating and has a magnetic pull. You'll hurry to nail that carpet back down to the floor, but you can never unsee what you've seen or unknow what you now know—which is that the whole world sits on a foundation of nothingness and there is just a very thin, scratchy, decades-old piece of budget carpet between you and it. Here's the trick. Although everything inside of you will want to run away from it, close your eyes to it, ignore it—the answer is actually to simply face it. To stare into the dark until you know its depths, until you get your bearings back, until you see the light.

So this is where Richie and I start our next session. Standing at the edge of the abyss. Together. This is the only way to battle all the numbness. To revive the feelings and feel some of them together.

> "Close your eyes and tell me what you see, Richie. I'm standing right next to you."
> There's a long pause, and I can feel the discomfort—near panic—that is pulsing through Richie's veins as he peers into the past he's been doing everything he can to forget. "My room in the dark. That awful feeling. It covers everything. Like snow, but black. Silent. Not exactly like snow. It covers over everything, but it's also inside of it. It's in my lungs. Sitting in the hospital room with my parents and my sisters. Everything is wrong, but they keep asking me what it is that's wrong and I can't point to any one thing. *Nothing* makes any sense. And it's just so sad. So sad."

Here are all the feelings that Richie has been so scared of; here's everything he swept under the rug. Each of the moments when the bottom dropped out and no one was there to catch him. Mom and dad splitting, his dream job not actually feeling like a dream, his dream girl walking out the door. If all these structures crumble, what's left? Life is meaningless. This is his dark. This is why he's numbing everything. To protect himself from that spot and this dark. It occurs to me that it's not actually the darkness that scares him. It's the memory of being plummeted into it the first time.

> "Hang on. Richie. Do you know that it's never going to be that bad again?"

Richie is looking at me now, wide-eyed like a little kid. His eyes are filling up with tears.

"What do you mean? That feeling is always right there, it's right outside the door. Always waiting to take over."

"Yes. That feeling is a part of the world. It's a part of your world. But you can only meet the abyss for the first time *once*. When you did, you didn't have any tools. You didn't know that the abyss even existed! That was *horrifying*. You know that it's there, and you know what to do when you feel like you're approaching it. You're going to encounter that abyss again. Life will make sure of that. But it's never going to be like that first time. Never. I promise. Because you know this dark. And you know exactly what to do when you find yourself there."

We gently swing out of the emotions because they are too intense to stick with. We go back to look at this from the safer ground of the intellect, and I tell Richie a little bit more about the existentialists.

The difference between the existentialists and everyone else is that they do not try and craft a thicker carpet and more industrial nails to better cover the abyss or create some huge ideological system to keep us busy and distract us from the fact that the world is not balanced on the back of a giant tortoise, and it is not held in place on the shoulders of Atlas—it is floating in deep, dark, empty space. They don't numb themselves against it. Instead, they thought the answer to the abyss and all the awful, wrenching feelings that come from its discovery is to simply stand there and face it. Keep pulling up the carpet. Accept it. OK, darkness. OK, great swirling abyss. OK, nothingness. I see you. Do you see me? Stare at it for long enough, and your eyes start to adjust.

The darkness will trick you into thinking that you are the very first person to have discovered it, but rest assured, none of us is alone here. Camus and the other existentialists and every other human that has ever been introduced to the abyss (so, all of them) are standing right there waiting, ready to say, "Hey, I know this looks a lot like the end, but it's actually the beginning." Because here's the thing—when you stare at the abyss for long enough for your eyes to adjust, you start to laugh. You find yourself laughing because suddenly you see that the world takes itself way too seriously. It's neither inherently good nor shot through with evil—it's *absurd*. Meaningless. Well, meaningless except for us. So what if life is built on a foundation of nothingness? Is that so terrible? Maybe. Maybe not. It's hard to know. But there's not a whole lot we can do about it. The heroic, absurd, irreverent, and subversive thing to do in the face of that abyss is to *live*. To make meaning in the nothingness, like a little girl splashing in a puddle and cackling like a hen.

Listen, you probably didn't put "make meaning out of nothingness" on your to-do list for today. It's a big ask. And it's a big ask if you're just bopping along having a regular Tuesday. It's a huge, daunting, impossible, nauseating task if you are facing the abyss in some way. Mental illness. A breakup. The loss of your job. Any other devastating blow. This is why we have to be so careful when we talk about the gift of meaning making. Because here's the final piece: you are free to make meaning, but *you don't have to.* You don't even have to go on living. It's always, *always* your choice, which means you are never trapped. When life really is too much, when the task of making meaning stops being feasible, you can make it all stop. Dark, I know. But do you see all that inescapable freedom right there in the darkness? The darkest thing that you can imagine is also the very thing that is holding up your freedom. Here's the most critical piece: That freedom exists not in spite of the darkness but *because of it.* There is a powerful and meaningful rebellion here that can arise only when all your hope and faith have been stripped away. The existential crisis is not the end—it's the starting gun.

Richie isn't suicidal anymore, but our work is not done yet. We're really just at the beginning. We still have to learn what to do with all these feelings and memories we are left with when we stop numbing. We're still standing at the edge of the abyss. Here's the thing that no one tells you about going through an existential crisis. Yes, everything you thought you knew gets obliterated. Yes, you are left shaking and stripped down and terrified like a baby bird that just got thrown out of its nest by her asshole big brother. And the foundation that you will build once you really know the nature of the world is a million times stronger than the one built on fluffy falsehoods and counterfeit hope.

FINDING YOUR WAY IN THE DARK

The problem with living in a society that cannot tolerate the darkness is that it ensures that none of us knows what to do when we get plunged into it. How to even recognize that we have gotten plunged into it. When we can't tolerate the darkness, we inadvertently send a message that when you are struggling with this kind of terror, you will have to grapple with it alone. And while you may not get plunged into Richie's specific darkness—you will get plunged into some kind of darkness. Talking about it can't save you from that, but it can prepare you for it. And being prepared is like having a hidden crossbody bag underneath your shirt. The thief can steal your backpack all he wants, but he won't get your passport, phone, credit card, or soul.

First, let's name this abyss-finding, this darkness-plunging, this tenacious street thief (name it to tame it, right?). It is an existential crisis. What's an existential crisis? It is what happens when you're faced with the abyss that undergirds existence itself. It is a profound and distressing psychological or philosophical experience in which you find yourself grappling with questions about the fundamental nature of your existence, the meaning and purpose of life, and your own place and significance in the world. To be clear, you will do your grappling with angst by your side. You will wade through uncertainty like it is quicksand and search for meaning like you are looking for water after three and a half days in the desert.

The abyss is a sneaky motherfucker, and sometimes you will get swept into it without realizing what's happening. You'll know you're in it if you find yourself questioning the meaning of life. If you're wondering why you exist at all. You might also suddenly feel gripped by your own mortality or mortality in general. If someone buys you flowers and your first thought is, "Why on earth would you buy me a bouquet of dead things?" you're in it. If you realize that you've lost a whole bunch of beliefs, or values, or systems of meaning that you previously held, if you feel untethered and utterly adrift, you're in it.

You're tuning out right now; I can feel it. "I get it, MC, it's dark down there. Is this enough yet?" I get it. And no. We're almost there, hang on. This is the thing that happens when we're faced with the darkness, whether it is our own or someone else's—we tune out too soon. We miss the second clause and think that life is just straight-up meaningless, and we miss the part where the existentialists say that suicide is not the answer.

Do you know the story of Chris McCandless? He is the person that *Into the Wild* was based on, an American adventurer who set out to conquer Alaska. In other words, he plunged himself into the darkness. And conquer Alaska he did. Until he got too weak to cross the Teklanika River to get back to civilization and died in the bus he was living in. Because Chris didn't have a map, and because he stopped searching, he missed the fact that there was a hand-operated cable car a half mile away that would have taken him across the river. He was a half mile away from a new beginning. Let's keep going.

Luckily for us, the cable car is right here in the existential crisis. Yes, this is a dark place. Yes, there is anxiety here. And there's also depth, and curiosity, and hope. These are three anchors that exist right here in the dark. And if we can see these, we can use them to build a new foundation.

When you get plunged into the dark, the *first thing* you'll find yourself doing is searching. Searching for the light, searching for a way out, searching for your own feet, searching for the ground. You'll find a bit of light as your eyes adjust, you'll find your own feet, and you'll find the ground. Once you place your palms down on it and orient yourself, you'll know which way is up, and so you'll also find the way out. Though you would no doubt reverse the circumstances that got you here, you'll feel grateful for the depth you've suddenly discovered. Because like it or not, you're growing. Richie's darkness—a darkness that I would spin the hands of time backward to protect him from if I could because I know just how painful it is—brought him to new depths. Depths that simply wouldn't have been possible without first being plunged into the dark.

The second thing that we find when we lean into the darkness is curiosity. When you find yourself in the middle of an existential crisis, you find yourself forced to really look at the way you are living. This can be a tremendous opportunity to make changes, reevaluate priorities, and evolve. Millions of us did this during the pandemic by quitting dead-end jobs and getting our drum kits out of storage. This often leads to huge mindset shifts, and people often find themselves in better alignment with themselves.

The third thing that we discover in the darkness—if we are open to it—is an unexpected joy in world building. This is where all the existential empowerment comes in. No, there's no inherent meaning in the world for us to search for and discover. Yes, that's scary. And also, this is exciting! It can be a huge new source of creative life energy. It means you get to paint whatever you want, and you cannot make a mistake. Existence is the ceiling of the Sistine Chapel, and you've got Michelangelo's brush. What do you want it to look like?

I am going to give you some tools that are built on these three things we find in the darkness, but first I want to wrap up Richie's story because I hate cliff-hangers, and I *really* hate surprises. It's been about four years since Richie's last suicide attempt, and we've talked every week. We've talked about philosophy, about work, about sadness and what exactly it feels like when it drapes itself over and inside everything in your life, about his family and his friends and his job, about the life that he wants to build for himself. We do this gently, slowly. Richie is no longer afraid of the dark. He's too busy rebuilding the world, every now and then turning to nod at the abyss, marveling at its absurd contradiction. It is both the thing that destroyed everything and the thing that made it possible for him to build all of this.

STEPS TO TAKE WHEN YOU FIND YOURSELF PLUNGED INTO THE DARKNESS

When we lean into an existential crisis, we find three key constructive things right there in the dark next to all the chattering angst. Here are three super simple exercises to get you anchored and started on your way. Remember, you might be facing this dark, swirling abyss on your own, but all the rest of us who have faced it are standing right here behind you, securing a rope to your waist.

Searching for Meaning

Meaning is a thing we make. It is a work of art we place on top of life's events to render them coherent, to get closure; to cope. Meaning does not return our loved ones to us, and it is not a fair exchange for the loss. It's a different kind of thing entirely. It's the anchor line that we throw into the sea when we find ourselves lost. It's a dynamic work of art—we can go back and change it whenever we want. Add color, take it away, switch mediums entirely, turn it into a song. Meaning making is our greatest power as human beings, and we don't prioritize it or practice it nearly enough.

Relabeling Your Files

Step 1) Pick something in your life that has challenged you or led you to really question your beliefs and values. The first time you do this exercise, it's a good idea to pick something from a long time ago that you feel you have processed and that isn't actively haunting you. You can do it again with something hairier once you get the hang of it.

Step 2) On a piece of actual paper, make a list of everything that experience took away from you: your self-esteem, your sense of humor, your ability to sleep through the night. Don't forget to breathe. Put that list aside.

Step 3) On a separate piece of paper, make a list of everything that experience *taught* you. That you are tougher than you thought, that you can handle loss, that you now know how to get yourself resources when you need help. Underneath that, make some notes about how these insights might guide your actions and decisions moving forward. Keep breathing.

Step 4) Get out a folder and put both pieces of paper in it. Now it's time to label the file. Instead of labeling it with the name of the event, pick a phrase and label it with what it *means*. Focus here on both. What did it take, and what did it teach you? So, instead of your divorce being labeled "Divorce: the reason I'm a failure," you might write, "Divorce: the super painful thing that set me free and taught me what I really deserve." If your life was a movie plot, what does this event mean in the larger picture? It's OK if you can't do this right away; it can take a long time. Just keep the folder somewhere you can see it and come back when you can.

Step 5) As time goes on, allow yourself to change the meaning on the folder. You can just put a new label right over the old one.

Resetting Your Values Control Panel

Imagine that somewhere in the cloud (that's where the internet is, right?) there is a control panel that allows you to manage your life values. It's one of those panels that has a bunch of odometer-looking instruments, so you can see where the dial is pointed between 0 and 10. The goal of this exercise is to think about three things: what your values are, where you are currently in relation to those values, and where you want to be.

Step 1) Create a list of your most important priorities. You need to have at least three and no more than ten. These might be things like your relationships, career, personal growth, health, community. These are your top life values.

Step 2) Next to each value, rate its ideal level of importance to you on a scale of 1 to 10. Don't worry about whether you're currently meeting that level or not.

Step 3) Now think about where you currently are in regard to this value and give that a score as well. Write that number next to the ideal number that you wrote down first. For example, you might rate your relationships at a 10, but only be currently investing in them at about a 6. Or you might rate your career at a 6, but currently be investing in it at 10.

Step 4) For priorities that no longer serve you or are misaligned with your values, brainstorm steps you can take to realign them, or develop new priorities that reflect where you want to go. Here are some examples to get you started:

Relationships: If you value relationships at a 10 but are currently investing at a 6, consider scheduling regular catch-ups with friends or family, joining a social club in your town, or simply being more present in your interactions.

Career: If your career is currently at a 10 but you only value it at a 6, think about delegating tasks, setting boundaries for work hours, or exploring a career shift that aligns more closely with your passions.

Health: If you want health to be a top priority but you feel you are underinvesting, you might start by planning regular exercise, cooking healthier meals, or setting aside time for mindfulness practices.

Personal Growth: If personal growth is a key value but you're not investing enough time in it, consider enrolling in a course, reading more books, or setting aside time for self-reflection and journaling.

Priority	Value	Current status	Alignments
Friendships	10	5	Text Sue every week; Join the Saturday morning postrun coffee club at the gym
Work	7	10	Don't check email after 6 p.m.; If you have work on the weekends, designate one hour in the morning
Etc.			

Bonus! Creative World Building

OK, friends, I'm going to give you an art project. Since some of you may flap around and whine and do the whole obligatory "but I don't have a creative bone in my body" thing, you can call this a bonus exercise. (But remember: We're in the abyss. So take two minutes and flap, then pull out that box of Crayolas.)

Step 1) Gather any creative materials that resonate with you—this could be anything from a pen and paper for writing, paints and canvas for painting, or instruments for composing music. Glitter? Bring it!

Step 2) Reflect on the concept that life has no inherent meaning except for what we create for ourselves. Consider what brings you joy, fulfillment, and a sense of purpose. What images, colors, sounds come up when you think about these concepts?

Step 3) Set a timer for twenty to thirty minutes, and in that time your only job on this earth is to create. Not edit, not doubt, just create. Use your chosen medium to express these concepts, and create something. Anything. This could be a piece of art, a story, a song, or any other form of creative expression. It can be representational or abstract. It doesn't have to be pretty or make sense to anyone else. This is for you, and you alone.

Step 4) Put it somewhere you can see it. This is visual proof that you are a meaning maker, a creator, and that you can create even when things are dire.

Before we move on to Part 2 of the book, I want to build a little world with you right now. So far the thieves we've covered are hypervigilance and emotional numbing. Only today did I realize that the word *vigil* is right in the middle of *hypervigilance.* This makes sense because vigil just means "to be awake to." We know that we can stay awake to fear and to anxiety because we do that all the time. Trauma leaves all the lights on 24/7 like it's a guard at Guantanamo Bay. But what if we held vigil to joy in the dark? To hope in our most desperate times? Our traumas try to trick us into thinking that joy, connection, meaning, and vulnerability are dangerous, incorrect, and silly. That trick is based on a good intention—your fear is trying to keep you safe and alive—but it's also based on a lie. Because you just don't need to be hypervigilant all the time. You just don't.

There's an underappreciated psychologist named Nina Bull, who did pioneering work in the field of emotion and how emotions get expressed and held in the body. She was interested in how the body and mind reflect one another and how this might be key to breaking people out of negative states. In her research, she would ask people to stay frozen in really constricted body positions—think coiled tightly in a ball with their hands clenched—and ask them to reflect on moments where they felt love, joy, or curiosity.[2] These people who certainly had felt joy, love, or curiosity couldn't access those feelings in those body states. Then she asked people to freeze in really open and joyful positions—think of someone raising their hands all the way up to the sky to give you a huge hug around the neck—and asked them to reflect on moments where they felt terror. Guess what? They couldn't.

We talked about awe a little bit in the last chapter, and I want to return to it and consider that awe is just unadulterated joy for an experience. Overflowing emotion that comes from witnessing something that makes you marvel at the unabashed miracle of the world. Did you know that when people have the opportunity to go into space and look at Earth from way, way, way up high, they almost always cry? It's a good feeling, but maybe it also involves grief for the world they just lost—the world about which they hadn't yet had this major perspective shift.

When people experience the most radical things that the

universe has to offer, they universally report feeling awe. What that means is that at its core, awe comes from being radically changed by something. You find yourself in awe when something happens to you that fundamentally changes your model of the world and leaves you in its wake confused and blinking. Do you see where I'm going? The best things in life bring us to the abyss, too. The abyss is scary however we encounter it—we just label it *exciting scary* when it's about the stars and *terrible scary* when it's about loss. Your nervous system doesn't know if you're trying your first bungee jump or thinking about letting the abyss win.

To tie all this together, what if we held vigil to joy and awe like we do to death and darkness? What if we allowed ourselves to become hypervigilant about awe, seeking it out everywhere like some kind of *awe-ssassin*? And in a world like that, what if we were welcomed to tell our darkest stories as if we were astronauts returning from space? What if we viewed this transformation as one that breaks things open into light instead of breaks things down into darkness? We are the meaning makers after all.

Oh, and Richie? I'm *so* proud of you.

And you there, dear reader, who has also faced the abyss? I'm proud of you too.

Let's keep going.

PART 2

JOY
FEAR

CHAPTER 4

Fear of Loss: Building Your Hope Circuit

I want to know the joy
of how you whisper
"more."

—Rumi

ONE OF THE THINGS WE GET SO VERY WRONG ABOUT JOY and hope is that we assume they are bright, shiny things fit for bright, shiny circumstances. What if joy isn't the opposite of darkness, but a kind of relentless, steely thing you find within it? What if hope isn't some light and airy concept, but a rebellion against terrible circumstances?

The first time I encountered that kind of steely, rebellious hope was the first time I fell in love, which happened to be with a boy who was dying. When I met Jeremy, he was already ten years into borrowed time. He had been born with a terminal illness and was not expected to live past age five. I still have a photo of him at five. He's wearing a tiny blue baseball hat and mugging for the camera—mouth open and full of food. Rebellious and laughing and supposed to be dead.

It's been twenty-five years, and I've never written about Jeremy. Well, not directly. I've written a lot about loss—both my own and other people's losses—and I think some of this has served as a proxy. It's easier to write about other losses than it is to write about this one. I've written more about the death of Ralph Waldo Emerson's son Waldo than I've written about Jeremy's, which feels impossible, but I think sometimes our silences say more than our words ever could.

Sometimes the dead become unnamable to us because to name them is to place them among things that can still be called. Emerson says that Waldo is like mist in the air, everywhere and nowhere, something and nothing. What is left of Waldo is absence. There is a wild contradiction here, and it's difficult to render. How do you articulate the presence of an absence? How can you possibly do justice to that contradiction and the life that is contained within it?

I met Jeremy in 1995. I was fourteen and at a hockey game and paying a lot less attention to the hockey and a lot more to high school boys that might have come to the game. At the snack bar, I met Dave. Dave had jet-black hair, a diamond stud in one of his ears, and a sideways grin that spelled trouble with a capital *T*. He had a motorcycle? He was *definitely* older than me. Seventeen? Eighteen? He didn't mention college. Seventeen? Oh, God, what if he was nineteen? I was looking for hints and trying to do the math while I gave him my phone number. He grinned. My mom was going to *kill me*.

Dave called me later that night after the game (we didn't have time to wait three days in the '90s). I grabbed the cordless phone halfway through the first ring and sneaked down to the basement. What was my cutoff going to be? Seventeen? Should I lie and tell him I was sixteen? How long could I keep *that* going? Just as I was about to open my mouth and ask him how old he was, he said, "Here, talk to my cousin Jeremy," and handed the phone to a boy much closer to my age with a gravelly voice and a contagious laugh.

"How old are you?" Might as well just get this part out of
the way.
"Fifteen. You?"
"Fourteen!" *The relief.*
"How come you didn't go to the game tonight?" I asked.
"Oh, I'm in the hospital."
"Oh no! Why?"
"Oh, it's not a big deal, I'm just here for a tune-up."

As I sat on the striped couch in my basement, Jeremy told me that he had cystic fibrosis (CF). CF is a progressive genetic disease that prevents the proper movement of chloride through the cell wall. As a result, the mucus that forms in various organs becomes thick and sticky. This might not sound like a big deal, but mucus is supposed to carry bacteria and germs *out* of the body. When it can't, the body holds onto these germs and bacteria, which causes frequent lung infections and even respiratory failure. "Tune-ups" are common for those who have CF. It usually means a one- to two-week hospital stay to manage flaring symptoms and control infections in the lungs, sinuses, and pancreas.

"Does it hurt? Are you afraid?"
He laughed.

It's been nearly three decades since that phone call, but the memory is closer and more vivid than this morning's breakfast. The basement was cold, and I snuggled under a down blanket as we talked. It was *way* past curfew, and I was supposed to be in bed. I had given my phone number to a stranger that night, and I still didn't know how old he was. Now I was talking to that stranger's cousin. Again, my mom was going to kill me. None of it mattered. This laughing boy with the gravelly voice was living on borrowed time, so there just wasn't any left over for my mom's bullshit rules.

Jeremy was tall and thin. He had mischievous and sparkly green eyes and olive skin that tanned in the summer while mine flushed red. Jeremy introduced me to rap music and paella, basketball and *Men in Black*. He used to lie across his bed and write his favorite lyrics in a spiral notebook that he kept under his nightstand. Our first kiss happened in my garage and lasted an hour and a half. Jeremy had a scar on his chest from a port-a-cath and worried a lot about whether it would freak me out. His worry felt sacred. I traced the smooth scar tissue gently with my fingertips and marveled at the way his beautiful skin had woven together around it, shiny and strong.

Everything about Jeremy's life was a contradiction, and everything about our relationship was, too. He was alive and shouldn't be, and we were simultaneously young and old. Serious and silly. We didn't have licenses or cars and had to be driven to meet up at the movies. A lot of our dates took place in the hospital. We watched movies and stole scrubs and condoms from the hospital supply closet, made out in stairways and bathrooms. We sat on the phone late at night talking about what cars we'd drive when we grew up, and how we'd decorate our house, and how physical desire felt a lot like literal thirst.

I was so full of love and faith and believed so wholeheartedly in miracles that I didn't have one ounce of doubt that we would live a long life together. That Jeremy would be cured. He wasn't. By now he's been gone for longer than he was here, and I don't remember his laugh. I have thirteen photographs of us, and one or both of us is laughing in eight of them.

I think back to my fourteen-year-old self often and with envy. She was *so* fearless, *so* committed. Now I'm haunted. The truth is that my first relationship was as much with the grim reaper as it was with Jeremy. And now that he is gone, I'm left with the specter of death, and it has haunted every single subsequent relationship in ways I've never even acknowledged. It's easy to tell a bright story about young love and young loss. It's less easy and a lot darker to admit that I have been stuck rehearsing future losses since I was sixteen. Since before my brain was fully formed. Since before my parents died.

Even though losing is the thing I've done more than just about anything else, I live every single relentless second of every single day gripped and terrified of loss. What does that mean? It means that when I look at an apartment listing with someone I love, the very first thing I imagine is what the kitchen is going to feel like the morning after they die. It means that if we're watching a movie together, I'm trying to concentrate on the movie instead of picturing you having a heart attack right here in the living room. It means I think about what questions I'm going to regret not having asked you more than I meal plan. It means that many, *many* nights I wake up and wonder if you've stopped breathing in your sleep. It's a sick and selfish worry, and it means that if I love you, I've planned your funeral.

And. Since I've been in a relationship with the grim reaper since I was fucking fourteen, I can tell you with certainty that even while you are choking on grief, there is still hope. I can tell you that right here in all this murky, muddy fear, there is also joy.

JOY IS A VERB, DAMN IT!

Let's step back for a moment and consider the word *joy*. Earliest uses place it in the 1200s when as a noun it meant "feeling of pleasure and delight." As a verb, though, the meaning is so much more revealing of its nature. It heralds from the Old French *enjoir*, which is, "to give joy, rejoice, take delight in." If we make noun-and-verb dance partners, what we get is "the feeling of pleasure or delight when you give, rejoice, take delight in." Joy is something that we *do*. Something that we take. Joy isn't inherently in something in the world, it isn't the random result of a set of circumstances—it is something that we take, render, and share. There's a rebellion there; joy feels like something stolen, something alchemical. I love this.

And hope? Buckle up. *Hope* comes from the Old English *hopian*, which is to "have the theological virtue of Hope; hope for (salvation, mercy), trust in (God's word)," or "to have trust, have confidence." In the 1600s, the word gets doused with darkness: "to hold hope in the absence of any justification for hope." To hope is to transcend one's circumstances—to know that the circumstances are dire and choose to dream anyway. It is to take on a certain disposition in the face of the unknown, even when the unknowing is unrelenting. It means to trust anyway, not in spite of impending doom, but precisely because of it.

Quick, someone embroider that on a throw pillow!

Jeremy's circumstances were shitty. Falling in love with a person who is terminally ill is shitty. There was no cure, and no justified reason to believe there would be a cure before his clock ran out. There still isn't a cure—although treatments have improved markedly, and folks tend to live a pretty full fifty or even eighty years. And. We found joy anyway. We stole joy from those shitty circumstances and polished it into this shiny, beautiful, soaring thing. We made it joyful. And we had hope. So much hope. My fourteen-year-old self wore her rebellious hope like a leather jacket with spikes, as if to say, "Yes, I am in love with this dying boy. Infinitely so. Yes, I have hope. Why wouldn't I?"

Because Jeremy helped me build my hope circuit.

THE HOPE CIRCUIT

If we want to understand how to work with the hope circuit, we need to understand more clearly what it is and what it does. So, let's start with some basic neuroscience.

It is a testament to the wild complexity of the human brain that any metaphor that we use to understand it completely falls apart at some point. When neuroscientists talk about brain circuitry, for example, they almost always use the metaphor of a series of interconnected roads. The image that always comes to mind for me is the 405 in LA, but if you've spent an afternoon or two on the 405, you know that it has a way of throwing you into an existential crisis. More important, the metaphor falls apart when you try to figure out in what way the roads are and are not like neurons. I'm going to simplify this and make it as clear as possible.

Think about your brain like a circuit board. All the different parts of the brain are wired together in circuits. These circuits are really important because when they fire up, they are what determine our thought process, belief, or behavior.

Each circuit requires energy in order to work, and our brain doesn't have unlimited energy. In some ways, you can think of the brain like an old house—in a house with an older electrical system, you can't run all your appliances at once because a fuse would blow. The brain is just like that—you can't run all operations at the same time; there's just not enough energy.

Certain circuits take a lot of energy and so they are counterposed—meaning if one is on, the other one cannot be on. Two circuits in the brain that we know to be counterposed are the hope circuit and the fear circuit. The fear circuit (sometimes called the limbic system, sometimes called the reptilian brain) is the circuit board that is responsible for processing emotions in general—but perhaps most important, fear responses, which take up a huge amount of circuit energy. It involves a couple of brain areas, but most notably the amygdala, which is an almond-shaped section of the brain that we have in common with fetuses and lizards.

The hope circuit also requires a huge amount of energy, but instead of danger and fear, it is involved in feeling connected to others, making decisions, planning for the future, and setting goals. This circuit involves a couple of brain areas as well—but most relevant is the prefrontal cortex. This is the part of your brain that develops last and is responsible for rational thinking, working memory, and other things. I like to think of it as the executive assistant of the brain—and it doesn't fully develop until you're thirty-plus.

The brain is miraculously adaptive and does not have unlimited energy, so to maximize efficiency, it makes sure the circuits that take a ton of energy don't run at the same time. Your house might be a little like this in that if you try to run your air conditioner and microwave at the same time, a fuse will blow. The hope circuit and the fear circuit work like this too.

When it comes to fear, you have likely experienced this many times. When you are super nervous about a presentation at work, or when you hear a noise in the middle of the night and are trying to determine whether someone is breaking into your house, you do not simultaneously start to plan your next vacation. When you are in a fear response, this would be absurd. We can see immediately how this is adaptive. A key reason that fear exists to begin with is to keep you pulled to *this* moment, *this* potential danger. For your brain, survival is job number one.

Here's the exciting part, though, the part that we almost always overlook. If it's hard to feel hope when we are steeped in fear, the reverse is also true. Yep: it's hard to access fear when we are steeped in hope. This is true neurobiologically— hope actually inhibits fear.

Wait, sorry, did you hear that? *Hope inhibits fear.*

Here's how: the amygdala is the center intersection of the circuit board that the fear circuit runs on—when we are afraid, *all* the energy goes shooting directly to it. The reason that happens is because the perception of threat sent a lot of neurotransmitters (little chemical messengers that send signals all around your body) shouting "DANGER!" and then many different parts of your brain and body got ready to fight. This was to get you prepared to handle the threat that is all up in your face.

We are not totally at the mercy of the whims of the amygdala. If the prefrontal cortex is online when the danger messages get sent, it can actually send inhibitory neurotransmitters that can slow down the "DANGER!" calls, which then slows down the fear response. This is how the prefrontal cortex can help regulate emotions—by modulating the intensity of neurochemical responses. Any time you reason with yourself about a fear that you're having, you are recruiting your prefrontal cortex to provide a rational and calming influence on your (often irrational) fear. This dampens the fear response and leads to a more balanced emotional state.

Maybe you send a text to your friend, and they don't respond. At first you don't think anything of it, but suddenly you notice that it's been four hours, and the fear circuit fires up. "Did I offend her last night with that joke about the porcupine?" You start checking your phone every minute and stop being able to concentrate. The prefrontal cortex gives you a reality check: "Yes, it's possible she's mad at you about that joke. But you've been friends for eleven years—you can likely repair this. It's also possible that she's in a meeting, left her phone at home, or just forgot to text you back because it's been a busy day." Fear signals get inhibited, and you start feeling more calm.

Pretty cool, right? It gets even better.

While we're talking about neurotransmitters—remember, little chemical messengers that send signals all around your body—you may be familiar with the neurotransmitters serotonin and dopamine. These two play a *major* role in motivation and mood regulation. (The second *S* in SSRI is short for serotonin—selective serotonin reuptake inhibitor.) Activation of the hope circuit causes the release of these neurotransmitters, which also dampen the neurochemical processes associated with fear and anxiety. What does this mean? Practically speaking, this means that way more of the fear and anxiety we feel are within our control than we might think. It means that when you think positively about a single, tiny thing, you are regulating your own brain away from fear and anxiety and toward balance.

Wait. Am I telling you that you are in charge of your own emotional reality? I am telling you that you are more in charge of it than you might think. Listen, before you lose your mind and start listing all the things that are not within your control, I know. I totally get it. And here's the thing: you're right. There is a lot that we are not in control of. Our circumstances largely get handed to us whether we want them or not. Jeremy was born with a terminal illness. There are threats and fears and terrible things that befall us out of the clear blue sky, and the fact that we all know this and go on living anyway instead of just collapsing in fear is one of the jagged and prickly miracles about being human.

And still. The rest of the story is that we have more say when it comes to how we deal with the circumstances that get set out in front of us. This is true whether we know it or not—but when we know it, we have way more say. The more you can connect to your hope circuit, the more grounded and regulated you will feel. The neuroscience is clear and simple on that, and further studies continue to show it to be true.

There are probably many more ways to connect to the hope circuit than we currently know, which is exciting. That means that as the research continues to unfold, we will have even more ways to regulate ourselves. I'm going to give you an exercise at the end of the chapter to practice, but first I want to tell you a story about how we sometimes access exactly what we need without knowing that we are doing it. Because that story is a kind of miracle we don't pay attention to enough—the miracle of automatic adaptation. We adapt without knowing what we are doing. That means that there is something within us that does that naturally.

When visiting hours were over at the hospital and we all had to go home, all the kids in the adolescent wing of the hospital were alone. The lights would dim and of course there were nurses on the hall, coming in and out and taking vitals. There were TVs (no smartphones then—believe it or not, we still had beepers in the mid-'90s) and there were your thoughts. It would have been really easy to pick up that fear circuit board and send those cars flying around the tracks on two wheels all night long.

Jeremy didn't do this. Instead—and he almost never talked about this—he spent those hours helping the other kids in the adolescent wing. He'd sit with them in their rooms or talk to them on the phone. Check in with them about their tune-up progress or the surgery they had coming up. He'd remind them not to give up or to give in to the fear. He'd make them laugh. Pass the time. Hope for their recovery. Cheer when they got to leave the wing without him.

He didn't know it then because neuroscience didn't even know it then, but he was building and accessing his hope circuit. One of the most sure-fire ways to fire up your hope circuit is simply to be kind to others. Think about what that says about how our little brains are wired. When we step out of ourselves and help someone reach something on a high shelf at the grocery store or pause for a moment and hold the door for someone carrying a lot of packages at the post office, our brains interpret the world as safe. The fear center powers down, and the hope circuit fires up.

It's so hard to describe the *presence* of someone because it's everything about them that tries to escape language. Jeremy had such a grip on what it meant to be alive that I think he probably felt like a guide to most everyone in his life regardless of how many years they might have on him. His presence was strong and grounding and settled and forward looking. Steadfast. This is pretty remarkable for a boy who is fifteen and dying.

Part of the reason that the loss of Jeremy was so large is because his hope circuit was mighty, and he was using it to help other people build theirs. He was teaching us all that though fear and anxiety can derail us, keep us small, ruin our relationships—we can still find ways to hope, to feel and spread joy, to connect. Even while we're in the hospital. Even while we're dying.

I'm still working on my fear of loss—I really meant it when I said I am haunted. But listen, this is going to be a real hard pill to swallow, so feel free to spit it clear across the room if you want to, but I have been through enough loss in my life to be able to definitively tell you that although grief is a real motherfucker, there's also joy within it. Nobody talks about that. We want it to stay dark, singular, terrible. But it's too rebellious and complex for that.

I have always sort of bristled at the statement "grief is just love with nowhere to go" (Jamie Anderson). I think it bothers me because it assumes two things. First, it assumes that once the object of love is gone, that there is nowhere it could possibly go. That's just not true. It gets redirected—to your memories, to yourself, to other people. It grows. Loss transforms love from a quality that you feel about a single person to something essential and universal. It gets bigger. Second, it assumes that once someone is gone, your relationship is over. This is also not true. Loss shores up your relationship in a way; it assures you that your relationship is never over.

There are a lot of contradictions in this story, and I know that can feel like tension, but it's also beautiful. Jeremy has been gone for a long time now. And he's still here. He inspired people in life and continues to after his death. You've just been reading about him, and he's helping you understand your hope circuit. And if we know this about our brain—that the hope circuit exists and that it dampens some of the fear we feel—then we are much more able to access it.

TINY GRATITUDE ACTS

I'm going to level with you here: I *hate* gratitude lists. I hate how popular they got and then immediately how empty they became. Whenever I tried to partake, it felt woefully disingenuous. I'd dutifully write, "I'm grateful for coffee, my clients, and the conversation I had with my oldest friend this evening." These things were true, but I would immediately remember that just yesterday I was complaining to my sister that the gratitude list feels like yet another thing to do and that I was also complaining about just how many of my clients *always* take those extra ten minutes after the fifty-minute session is actually done—those precious ten minutes that I really needed to catch up on notes, take a breath, and pee—to tell me the really crucially important stuff, and that I was really irritated when Jen called after dinner because I'd been talking all damn day. I'm not saying that we can't feel gratitude for things that irritate us, of course, but it always felt a little bit like I was just checking a box here and making a list of things that I should be grateful for instead of actually feeling gratitude.

We can still start with this list, though. We just need to take it one or two steps further. First, by activating something called *felt sense*, and second, by turning gratitude into an act of kindness. These two steps ensure that the hope circuit is lit up in two ways—first, there is the imprinting of the gratitude, and second, the act of kindness toward someone else.

Felt sense is a bit hard to describe because what it aims at is the way that something lands in your body before language gets hold of it. It's important, though, because it connects your mind to your body and fills out a concept with a whole new layer of feeling. I can tell you in words about how much I loved rolling down the hill behind the lacrosse fields when I was a little kid: when I was a little kid at my brother's lacrosse games, I used to climb up the hill behind the fields and roll down it, laughing. Here's the same story with felt sense: When I think about rolling down the hill behind the lacrosse fields when I was a little kid, the first thing I remember is the distinct feeling when I reached the part of the hill that switched from sand to grass. I could feel it even though I was going too fast to see where I was. It went from slow and soft to slippery and fast, and there was a moment of breathlessness right before I came to a stop at the bottom. The sky looked wobbly, and the ground felt so stable while I let hilarious, bubbling dizziness wash over me. No matter how long I lay there in the grass and waited for the world to stop spinning, when I got up my knees still felt a little like Jell-O. See what I mean? When I tell the story this way—I can feel it.

I can make a gratitude list that is flat and empty: I'm grateful for this time to write, for this can of limoncello LaCroix, and for last night's nine-hour sleep. All of those things are true on that list, but making it is going to have pretty limited impact. Not zero impact, but pretty limited.

So, let's supercharge it.

SUPERCHARGED GRATITUDE

Step 1) Make a list of three things you are grateful for that have to do with other people. These things might be specific things that people have done for you today (a friend checked in to ask how you were doing, your spouse did the grocery shopping for you, your mom sent you that meme that made you laugh), or they might just be qualities in other people that you admire.

Step 2) Starting at the top of the list, pause for thirty seconds and try to really sink into the way that gratitude feels in your body. Don't worry about words and images—if they come up, that's fine. If not, that's fine too. Just focusing on *feeling* it. What is that feeling like from the inside out?

Step 3) Repeat this for each of the things on your list—pausing for at least thirty seconds each. Doing this ensures that making the list actually lands in your body and changes what can become a mindless task into something more alive and dynamic.

Step 4) Take at least one of the things on your list and turn it into a little note and send it along to the person whom you are grateful for. Send that note. And resistance? I see your hand up, and I already know your question. Sometimes the people you are most grateful for aren't there to send a text to anymore. Write it anyway.

When I was embarking on this chapter, I knew I was headed into a bit of a dark cave and one that I hadn't visited on purpose in a very long time. So, I made sure to gather supplies before I set off. I pulled out old photos and notes, and I made a playlist of all the songs I could think of from that time. I just went searching for memories, but I found a lot more than I bargained for. Yes, there was ache and longing, regret and a heavy kind of sadness that felt like it was pulling on time. And there was also my prom dress, which I had somehow forgotten looked just like a wedding dress. And all the words to "Wild Thing" by Tone Loc and "Big Pimpin'" by early days Jay-Z. And such vast gratitude for that relationship, and this loss—this one that shapes and sometimes limits me. Yes, the fear of loss, and yes, the gratitude. Yes, the sorrow, and yes, the joy.

And Jeremy? *Thank you.*

CHAPTER 5

Fear Conditioning: Joy When Joy Is Triggering

Embracing our vulnerabilities is risky but not nearly
as dangerous as giving up on love and belonging and
joy—the experiences that make us the most vulnerable.
Only when we are brave enough to explore the
darkness will we discover the infinite power of our light.

—Brené Brown

REMEMBER CHRISTINA? SHE'S THE CLIENT WHO TOLD ME to go fuck myself and slammed her computer shut when I suggested that she needed some levity in her life. There's no doubt that part of the reason she was so resistant to this was because of my own relational failure. It was as if she were trying to tell me that she was drowning, and I responded with, "Well, have you ever tried water aerobics?" I had suggested joy at the worst possible moment, and she felt dismissed and unheard.

Another reason she rejected this suggestion is that she was probably thinking of joy as the superficial kind that glints falsely on the surface of suburban wine tumblers. She was far too accustomed to the dark to believe in *that* kind of joy. But there's something deeper in her resistance. I know this because I've seen it in other clients and in myself. It's also right there in the intensity of her response.

This is not at all to say that her response was wrong—not at all. But her response is relevant. Christina could have responded in any number of ways. She could have laughed and asked for an explanation. She could have said, "Are you kidding me?" and left enough silence for me to say more. She could have sat back in her seat without saying anything and raised an eyebrow. But she raged instead. The fact that she was so quickly enraged suggests that her fight/flight/freeze response was activated. Was joy the trigger? If so, why? And if she had continued to work with me, what could we have done about it?

WHAT EXACTLY IS A TRIGGER?

There is no official or clinical definition of the word *trigger*, so we need to build a definition for ourselves. In the most general terms, when we talk about "being triggered," what we most often mean is that something unexpected has happened that evoked an extreme negative response—one that takes us out of the moment and leaves us flooded or frozen or ready to run.

In some cases, that unexpected thing is something external to us, and it has a cascading negative effect internally. So, the fluorescent lights in your office might trigger a migraine, resulting in twenty-four hours of pain, nausea, and sensitivity to light. Hearing your wedding song in a department store three months after you sign your divorce papers might trigger sadness, resulting in sudden tears in public, and then embarrassment as you hide in the dressing room waiting for the wave of grief to roll over you.

This definition is a bit thin. In the field of trauma, the word *trigger* was originally supposed to refer to a unique neurobiological event. Namely, when something in our perception evokes a memory that hasn't been processed properly. This causes that memory to come surging forward as an instance of reliving instead of remembering.

Imagine a veteran who has just returned from combat is walking down a quiet street when suddenly a car backfires. To most people, the sound is just loud and startling, but to the veteran, the sound is not just noise; it's a memory capsule. The pitch of the car backfiring is the exact same as that of gunfire, and this life-threatening sound evokes a flood of memories from deployment. Instead of simply remembering the events as past occurrences, the veteran feels as though they are happening right here and now.

It's critical to understand that this is not a conscious choice or some kind of cognitive failure to distinguish the past from the present. It's a completely unique neurobiological event where the brain and body experience the threat as immediate. Your heart races, you taste metallic adrenaline in your mouth, your fight or flight response is fully activated—all because a part of your brain has equated the sound of a backfiring car to mortal danger.

This kind of memory is hard to talk about because in some very real ways, it isn't a memory. At the very least, it's not a memory that follows the rules. Regular memories can be brought into cognitive awareness, sifted through, and then put away with relative ease. And all throughout that process, we have the conscious understanding that the contents we were sifting through happened in the past. Triggers, on the other hand, bypass the rational parts of the brain and directly evoke an immediate and intense response. The response is overwhelming, often disproportionate to the triggering event itself, precisely because it is not about the present moment but a past memory that has not been fully processed and integrated.

Happy memories also evoke the past, but in a completely different way. Imagine, for example, that you walk into a coffee shop on a rainy March afternoon with a friend, just as the barista is placing a tray of freshly baked cookies in the display case. The smell of warm brown sugar makes you think of sitting on the counter while your mom taught you how to soften up the brown sugar in the microwave when it had crystalized in the cupboard. You might share this vivid memory with your friend, getting a little bit lost in it while you share. You might decide to buy the still-warm cookie even though it's not paleo. You would likely feel some emotions as you sifted through the memories. Nostalgia, contentment, maybe a burst of joy. The rational part of your brain stays connected, and so when you step up to the counter, you would be able to set the memory and feelings down and refocus on what you had wanted to order. We might say that these memories were "triggered" by the stimuli—meaning the smell of cookies evoked the memory of childhood—but you wouldn't say that you had been triggered. That's because the nature of trauma memories is so different. In fact, they shouldn't even be called memories at all.

When we think about triggers, we tend to place the negative nature of the trigger in the stimulus and assume that we are triggered by "bad" things. That's one of the reasons I used such clichéd examples just now. Combat memories are triggering; cookie reveries are not. This gets a lot more confusing when we are triggered by things that are not universally considered "bad" or "traumatic" in nature. This is because the nature of a trigger does not lie in the stimulus; it lies in the nervous system of the person being triggered. And we can be triggered by absolutely anything—including things that other people would not label as bad or scary. Yep, even cookies.

Imagine that your mother resorted to force feeding you when you were a child. She was concerned that you were becoming a picky eater, that you weren't getting the nutrients you needed to grow, and so she resorted to whatever means necessary while you screamed and cried and gagged. You might not even have a conscious memory of this because you were so young, but you feel anxious any time you have to sit at the dinner table to eat and find yourself eating at the kitchen counter or on the couch. Dinner is not inherently bad, nor are dining room tables. The fact that they trigger you has nothing to do with what they *are* and everything to do with what they *mean*.

All triggers are triggering because of fear conditioning, and believe it or not, fear conditioning is a neat adaptive response that likely evolved as a set of protective reactions to help keep us alive. Basically, when the brain receives signals that indicate threat, it initiates a set of reactions that makes it possible to better handle that threat. This is not a result of conscious exertion; in fact, the response happens before conscious input is even *possible*. This is a good thing, because some situations are so urgent we don't have the time to wait for conscious input before we act.

When this happens once, we have a singular adaptive behavior. I was staying at an Airbnb for a conference once, and the alarm system went off. It was a little cottage and had one of those fancy systems that can detect all sorts of different kinds of property breaches and will tell you exactly what's going on and call the police for you while you hide. So, it started shouting "living room window break, living room window break" in between loud ringing alarms. Within about two seconds and without thinking or deciding what my next move would be, I had instinctively grabbed my phone and dashed across the room into the kitchen, cowering behind some cabinets. My brain received stimuli that suggested a threat, processed the stimuli, and initiated the response. (It turned out to be a window sensor that had come unstuck.)

When this happens consistently and repeatedly, a singular adaptive response can become a default behavior, almost like a mental muscle memory. This is also adaptive—even though it can result in what we would call intrusive symptoms. It occurs because our brains are conditioned by what we experience. If you've ever heard of Pavlov's dogs, you've heard of conditioning. In the early 1900s, Ivan Pavlov famously discovered that the salivary reflex in dogs could be conditioned by repeating a specific sound each time food was presented. It was originally thought that the salivation response would only occur in the actual presence of food. What the experiment showed was that eventually, the dogs would salivate in response to the noise regardless of whether food was present. This seemed to prove that the salivation response in the brain could be conditioned to a previously neutral stimulus, which in turn suggested that the brain's automatic responses, though not conscious, could be trained.

In 1920, the psychologist John Watson conducted an experiment to see if fear was something that can also be conditioned. In his experiment, Watson aimed to see if he could create a fear of rats in a nine-month-old boy whom he called Little Albert. (You have to picture a cute white pet rat, here, not a six-pound NYC subway rat.) When Albert played with the rat, happily at first, Watson would make a loud clanging noise. The boy quickly came to associate the obnoxious noise with the rat and went from playing happily with it to refusing to go near it and crying when it was nearby. Watson also wanted to test the staying power of the response, and so he had Albert come back in a month to see if he would still respond in a fearful way to the rat, which he did. In a remarkably short time and because of the repetition of frightening negative feedback in the form of loud clanging, Albert's brain had created a fear response where one did not previously exist.

The takeaway? Well, there are two. First, triggers are a unique neurobiological experience that cause us to bypass our rational minds and act before we have any conscious input. You can't think your way out of a trigger. We should pay attention to when this happens—when we notice ourselves acting without thinking—and especially if the action seems more intense than the situation calls for. We should pay attention because there are only two reasons that this would happen. Either we are actually in danger, or we have labeled something benign (or even good) as danger. Because the thing that determines whether something is a trigger for us is the meaningful experience we have around it—not the thing itself. Second, this means that we can be triggered by anything, even joy.

CHRISTINA: TRIGGERED BY JOY

Christina walked on eggshells before she crawled. She was born an only child to a mother whose grip on reality was as fragile as a soap bubble. Her mother displayed all the signs of schizophrenia but lived in a religious culture that didn't believe in mental illness, so she went entirely untreated. Christina's father, exhausted by the constant caretaking, sought solace in the kind of echoless oblivion that can only be found at the bottom of a bottle of Jim Beam.

The top three emotions available to tiny Christina were uncertainty, terror, and longing—specifically, an aching longing for normalcy and love. Home was a dark labyrinth of extreme emotions; one moment would be eerily quiet and peaceful, and then without warning, the next was all breaking glass and crazed shrieking. Christina's mother could be a woman of profound kindness and incredible intelligence. However, these moments were fleeting. The tendrils of schizophrenia often wrapped around her mind, twisting her reality into one that was incommunicable and unrecognizable. Since no one was allowed to acknowledge that the mother's illness was real, the whole house followed the oscillations of her mind as if she were some psychedelic Pied Piper.

As children do, Christina found respite in the small, unremarkable moments—the quiet after an indoor storm, the fleeting warmth of the sun on a cold day. These moments were tinged with a profound sense of fear because they were always, *always* followed by something terrible. Joy became a harbinger of sorrow. Like her mother's psyche, it was a trick, a delicate soap bubble that would burst at any moment, leaving her hopeless and humiliated. She learned early to distrust happiness, viewing it as a precursor to disaster. If joy dared to enter her heart, it was quickly escorted out by her parents' next breakdown or outburst.

Once, when Christina was in the sixth grade, Christina's mother suggested that she invite some classmates over for a fancy tea party. They would dress up and decorate cupcakes with Wilton wedding cake decorations and sit at a beautifully set dining room table like European royalty. Christina's mother made intricate invitations and bought all the supplies, including a tablecloth covered in hand-painted roses. Every time Christina walked through the dining room, she ran her fingers across the roses, imagining the lovely afternoon they were about to have and the friendships that would be forged forever. The night before, Christina's mother invited her into the walk-in closet to try on clothes—somewhere Christina was never allowed to play—and began regaling her with stories of how all the girls' mothers were plotting against her. Christina felt special to be included in this adult world and was fascinated by the complex dynamics that seemed to center on her beautiful mother. It wasn't until years later that Christina realized that this elaborate social dynamic was a fabrication, a result of the paranoia that was the first sign of a psychotic episode psyching itself up in the wings.

By the time her classmates arrived, Christina's mother had unraveled entirely. She was crying into the cupcake batter and slashing at her clothes and hair. When Christina tried to calm her down, her mother threw a tin of silver dragées across the dining room and took off running through the yard barefoot and screaming while Christina's classmates stood stunned and scared. That was the last time Christina invited any would-be friends over. (Even now, at thirty-three, she still never invites anyone over.) In her brain, joy was becoming fused with disaster. At least the solution for that problem was easy enough—stay away from joy, and you will skirt disaster.

As Christina grew older, she sought to escape the chaos of her childhood and replace it with stability, structure, and a homey kind of rigidity. Partying in high school or college was not something that she had time for or found interesting. She was too busy studying her way out of her small town. She threw herself into her school, into work, into any endeavor that could offer a semblance of control. Relationships were navigated with a kind of caution that bordered on avoidance, and the fear of inheriting her mother's illness haunted her relentlessly through her twenties, when schizophrenia tends to present. Her peers aimed for happiness—something that she met with a raised eyebrow, hands on hips. It's not that she judged them for it; it's more that happiness felt like a puzzle she couldn't solve, a language she couldn't understand.

And then she met Dan. He was a full-time engineer, part-time artist—an intoxicating mix of structure and excitement. He was romantic and fearless, but also logical and clearheaded. He loved seeing live music and staying up late, but he seldom missed a day of work. Seeking expansion, not oblivion, he was more into weed and mushrooms than alcohol. He felt safe, and he made Christina laugh. Their dating years were idyllic—double features at the movie theater, restaurant tours of new cities, big stadium concerts, and cozy nights at quaint pubs. They traveled and laughed and argued a bit and moved in together and seemed like the perfect pairing of opposites. Christina grounded Dan, and Dan helped Christina let go just . . . enough. They had two little girls and moved to the suburbs. And that's when the wheels started to come off.

After each birth, Christina was gripped with postpartum anxiety. All the things that had initially attracted Christina to Dan started to grate on her. He didn't feel fearless to her anymore; he felt reckless. He wasn't as worried about the girls as he should be, didn't watch them closely enough, didn't care about the schedule, didn't see why it had to be so rigid. She started to feel like he couldn't do anything right and became intensely critical. They fought bitterly about the dishwasher—how it should be loaded and unloaded and when. Dan could not understand what had happened, why he suddenly stopped being able to make her laugh. He felt his wife slipping away and wrote her long letters, hoping to bring her back from this cold, dark place she seemed to go. She started to hate his relaxed nature, his ability to sit on the couch while the girls played and watch TV, his inability to worry about the dishes piling up in the sink.

In one session, seething, Christina describes an evening where she found herself standing in the kitchen, staring into the living room at Dan with a kind of hatred that felt like it was boiling her from the inside. She was cleaning up after dinner—nobody else could do it right, so she threw everyone out of the kitchen as soon as they were done eating—and Dan was sitting on the couch. Just sitting. He wasn't reading, watching anything, or playing a game. The girls were on the floor playing, and he was just sitting.

"I could never do that," Christina tells me. "Just sit there. Like a fucking rock. I'm in the kitchen, cleaning and cleaning after a ten-hour day and an hour of food prep and cooking and . . . He's. Just. Sitting. With this moronic grin on his face while he watches the girls." The contempt Christina has for Dan is a little bit shocking; it has so much electricity it could light up Dubai. But her contempt isn't really about Dan at all—and it may be contempt now, but it started out as envy. And we can be envious only about things that we do not have. What is it that Dan has that Christina so sorely lacks? The ability and the freedom to relax. To sit on the couch doing nothing other than watching their children play.

Emotions sometimes simmer. There are only two outcomes to simmering. They either stay simmering and then cool, or they come to a full rolling boil and transmute into other emotions. Depression can be like this; it simmers and simmers and can boil into rage and irritation. The same can happen with fear. Christina has been experiencing a simmering fear all her life, and now that manageable fear has bubbled into boil-over rage. She doesn't see this now, but she doesn't actually hate Dan; she is afraid. Her envy is rooted in fear. Joy and everything that comes with it—hope, rest, faith, giddiness—are threats, and the fact that Dan doesn't see that makes her feel unsafe with him and wildly alone. As alone as her mother, who lived in her own terror-ridden reality.

Remember—we can be conditioned to fear anything, and we can become afraid of joy in two distinct ways. We already know the first: for Christina (and many of us) joyful things happened right before terrible things, and so our brains make a false connection between them, labeling joy as a danger and teaching us to avoid it at all costs.

This avoidance feels like control and gives us the illusion that we are in charge and as long as we stay that way, nothing bad can happen. Conversely, when we do forget to avoid, any resulting pain or problem is our own fault. In Christina's developing brain, the anticipatory joy about the fancy tea party in the sixth grade was her own mistake. The narrative cannot be that her mother is mentally ill and desperately needs care because, while true, no one will cosign that truth, and this is not something that Christina can control. When we can't exert any power over something terrible, we sometimes make it our fault, our mistake. Because that way, we just need to figure out what's wrong with us and how to fix it, and we can change the course. Christina's brain searches for the circumstances that were under her sixth-grade control and comes up with the idea that the mistake she made was letting the hope in in the first place. She really should have known that this joy and that hope were misguided. Maybe if she hadn't been so blinded by the hope, she would have seen her mother's night-before paranoia as a sign of what was to come and canceled the event before her classmates witnessed the dark and terrible reality of her home life. Joy isn't experienced as a relaxation, a respite; it's a threat, a harbinger, a canary in the coal mine of her eleven-year-old heart.

FEAR CONDITIONING AND THE SNAPBACK EFFECT

The second way that we can become joy averse is a little more indirect and has to do with the way the nervous system learns this equation:

joy = danger

Think first about everything that joy might do in your body if you were to let it take over. Joy is an opening, a letting go, a release. Think about what it might be like to sit in a coffee shop and let yourself surrender to a daydream. Your shoulders will come down from your ears, your jaw will unclench. Your gaze will become soft as you stare into space, imagining. You might half-smile as ideas and images float into your consciousness, building on each other. You probably become so enamored with your little dream that you don't notice the man suddenly standing too close to you. You'll miss it entirely when he grabs your purse and tears out of the café with it. Wait, what? Shit. See?! This is what joy does—it leaves you vulnerable to the world you should have known was just getting ready to headbutt you. You should have known. You did know! You just let yourself slip. This is on you.

Given enough joy experiences that have an awful aftermath like this one, and your brain and body learn to reject joy without your input. It just cuts out the middleman. This is next-level fear conditioning, and you experience less and less of it, and for smaller and smaller snippets of time. You feel calm, you're basking in the loveliness of that calm, and then suddenly your brain and body remind you that the world is terrifying, and you'd better go back to paying attention. Or else.

This is an example of what is called the snapback effect in medicine. The snapback effect is a phenomenon where symptoms that are being alleviated or managed through a particular treatment suddenly reemerge with increased severity. Think of a bacterial infection that is being treated with antibiotics. Often patients experience a marked improvement in symptoms within twenty-four or forty-eight hours. If the bacteria develop resistance, however, the infection will come roaring back with symptoms worse than the initial ones. The explanation for the snap-back is pretty simple when it comes to things like bacteria. The bacteria got smarter, and the battle that looked like it was about to be won suddenly turns.

This is trickier when we are looking at treatments in the realm of psychology. Why would a patient who is becoming less depressed or anxious on a treatment plan suddenly experience a snapback? Historically, patients have been blamed for this—there was simply no rational explanation that would reveal why a treatment would work so well and then suddenly stop. What current science shows is that this snap-back might be due to the nervous system reacting against the therapy—not because it isn't effective, but because it is.

Like I said: tricky.

To understand this, we need to grab two quick concepts from biology: homeostasis and allostasis. One of the miraculous, amazing things that our bodies do without us even having any say is maintain homeostasis. This just means that the body is able to maintain a stable internal environment despite external changes. Various systems in the body do this by constantly regulating functions such as temperature, blood pressure, and hormone levels to ensure optimal conditions for the body's cells and organs to function efficiently. Our bodies are always aiming at homeostasis. They do this all the time, even when we're sleeping, and without our conscious input. Give your body a round of applause; this is pretty critical (and thankless) work.

Allostasis is how your body maintains homeostasis amid changing circumstances. Essentially, this is the process by which the body responds to stressors by overhauling physiological systems to maintain a baseline. Right now, if you're sitting on your couch reading this, you're probably not sweating. If you get up and take a brisk hike in the sun, your body will respond to the change in activity, heat, and humidity by releasing sweat to regulate your body temperature. If homeostasis aims to keep all your systems in a constant state, allostasis involves adapting to new circumstances by up-regulating or down-regulating the baseline in order to ensure the body is able to stay relatively stable through change.

The body is always aiming at homeostasis, even when you have an illness or condition. When you have something like anxiety, for example, your body adjusts to it over time through allostasis. People who have had a true panic attack can usually remember the event with laser accuracy and in excruciating detail. "I was walking through my living room and suddenly got completely filled with such an intense sense of dread that I dropped to my knees. My pulse raced, my skin burned, and I nearly called 911 because I thought I was having a heart attack." This is partly because the physiological experience of a panic attack is such a huge deviation from the norm. Over time, and with more attacks, your body raises homeostasis to account for these new physiological experiences. This might mean that you have a higher resting heart rate than you did five years ago before you were dealing with anxiety. Your body is trying to adjust to shifting circumstances and remain as efficient as possible.

Although this is your body's way of adapting—which is critical, and lifesaving—it has some side effects. For example, the longer you have something like anxiety, the harder it becomes to treat because your system has adjusted to it and will try and snap back to the new anxiety norm that it has grown accustomed to. For example, let's say you start taking an anti-anxiety medication like Xanax. This medicine automatically increases the amount of GABA in your brain, which helps you feel calmer within minutes (GABA, or gamma-aminobutyric acid, is a neurotransmitter that helps to calm the central nervous system). The problem is that your body has grown accustomed through allostasis to a higher heart rate, so as soon as the drug starts to wear off, it tries to help you by pinging your heart rate back up to where it was before, and boom—rebound panic, which many (myself included) report as feeling worse than the anxiety that the drug was aiming to quell in the first place.

This might sound backward, but it's just your body trying to help. When a treatment effectively reduces symptoms, it also inadvertently disrupts the body's established equilibrium, to which it has adapted over time, even if this equilibrium was pathological. The body's attempt to restore its original state can trigger a rebound effect, leading to the resurgence of symptoms. This is especially likely if the condition that is being treated has been present for an extended period. The nervous system has become adjusted to the condition—that elevated condition is now homeostasis—and will resist effective treatment by manifesting a snapback. Your body tries to help by interpreting the treatment as the problem, almost like a mental-emotional autoimmune disorder.

So, this makes sense when we're thinking about medications and conditions, but joy aversion is not a disease, and joy is not medicine. Right? Not so fast. Let's look at what joy does to the body, brain, and nervous system.

In the brain, joy triggers the release of several neurotransmitters and hormones, such as dopamine, serotonin, and endorphins. Dopamine gives us feelings of pleasure, achievement, and satisfaction. Serotonin stabilizes our mood and helps us feel happiness and contentment. Our endorphins—natural painkillers—elevate mood and reduce discomfort. In the body, joy leads to a decrease of stress-related hormones like cortisol and epinephrine—which lowers blood pressure, increases immune system response, and relaxes muscles. In the nervous system, joy activates the parasympathetic nervous system, which is responsible for the body's "rest and digest" responses. This activation counteracts the sympathetic nervous system's "fight or flight" reactions to stress, leading to a state of relaxation and balance.

So, joy and all its sister emotions *are* kind of like a medicine. And precisely a kind of medicine that happens to counter stress. If joy is a medicine and stress is a disease, a chronically stressed system can absolutely induce a snapback effect to joy.

When a traumatized and hypervigilant individual begins to

experience moments of joy, these positive emotions can initiate significant changes in their body and brain. As we've seen, joy can momentarily lower guard, reduce stress-hormone levels, and activate the parasympathetic nervous system, promoting a sense of peace and safety. However, this shift can also be startling for a system conditioned to constant alertness, a.k.a. hypervigilance. The sudden contrast between states of hypervigilance and relaxation can trigger a snapback effect, where the individual's nervous system quickly reverts to its previously heightened state of alert. Again, it's critical to remember that this is a protective mechanism—a response learned over time to avoid vulnerability that could come from lowering one's guard. But in our case, it's getting in the way by convincing Christina that Dan is dangerous and either his behavior has to change, or he has to go.

There's nothing wrong with Christina—in fact, her body is trying to protect her. The snapback effect is real, and it is tricky, but it is not the end of the story. This is not hopeless. If your system adapted to hypervigilance, stress, and anxiety, not all is lost. Why not? Because your system adapted to hypervigilance, stress, and anxiety. Your system is *adaptive*. We just have to get it adapted to joy—stat!

PENDULATION AND TITRATION

Have you ever seen that HBO show *In Treatment*? It's a scripted show about a psychotherapist, and each episode is a session with a different client. In the opening credits, the camera focuses in on a wave machine that sits on the therapist's shelf—a piece of kinetic art that is designed to simulate ocean waves. Picture a rectangular clear box with blue liquid in it. It sits on the shelf, and the base tips back and forth on a never-ending seesaw. Inside, the blue liquid perpetually sloshes gently back and forth, back and forth.

At first you might tag this as just set-design ephemera—an updated version of Newton's cradle (that's the desk toy with the silver balls that click back and forth—you've seen it because it's on every therapist's desk in film and TV history). But over time, you'll see how much work this object does. It's not only present in the opening credits, but it also anchors every episode and follows the characters through change. Over time, it comes to symbolize the ebb and flow of each session, the change that both the patients and the therapist go through, the cycle of emotions. It's also a perfect image to keep in mind here, because the movement at the core of this symbolic desk toy is the same movement we need to employ in order to heal from joy aversion—pendulation.

Peter Levine created the modality Somatic Experiencing therapy to treat trauma. With an understanding that the body has a natural rhythm and that healing from trauma must be slow and sustained, Levine crafted a system of healing methods that include pendulation and titration.

Pendulation involves the careful and mindful oscillation between states of activation and calm—think of the movement of a pendulum. This might be best understood by briefly looking at an opposing modality. In Prolonged Exposure therapy (the gold standard treatment for PTSD in the US), patients are guided to talk through a trauma memory in vivid detail with their eyes closed. The session is recorded, and the patient is instructed to listen to it over and over between sessions. The idea is that, over time and with enough sustained exposure, the memories lose their intensity and stop being triggering. From a theoretical perspective, this modality makes some sense. From a lived experience, the therapy is often compared to torture, tends to make patients suicidal, and has the highest dropout rate of any intervention designed to treat PTSD (50 percent).[1] Pendulation takes a completely opposing tack, gently invoking activating memories, tracking how those memories express themselves in somatic (bodily) symptoms, and then quickly guiding the patient back to safety. Not only is it a kinder method, but it also leverages the body's inherent ability to seek balance and healing and accepts that if an intervention is employed with too much force, it is likely to snap—or snap back in this case. In fact, pendulation actually accounts for a snapback, and has a built-in method for guiding the patient back to a calm and safe space when that happens, making sure that this doesn't render the treatment completely useless.

For someone joy averse, pendulation might involve initially bringing to mind a slight sense of pleasure or a happy memory—something as simple as the warmth of sunlight on their skin or the taste of their favorite fruit. As they notice any arising discomfort or resistance, which is not only normal here but desired, the individual then shifts their focus back to a neutral or grounding sensation, like the feeling of their feet on the cool hardwood floor. Then, once they are grounded for a few minutes, back to the happy memory. This back-and-forth motion, like the gentle arc of the wave machine, helps the nervous system become accustomed to the sensation of joy without being overwhelmed, facilitating a gradual reacquaintance with positive feelings. Since this is done slowly, the nervous system can engage in a kind of gentle allostasis, gradually becoming accustomed to a less hypervigilant way of life.

Titration is a word you might recognize from medicine. Sometimes patients are titrated to a drug; i.e., a clinical dose of a drug will be broken down into much smaller dosages that are given over time so the patient can get accustomed to it. It can be done in the opposite direction as well, so rather than a drug being stopped cold turkey (which can sometimes cause life-threatening withdrawal), patients will take a little bit less over time until they eventually stop entirely. Psychologically, titration is the process of exposing oneself to small, manageable doses of emotional or sensory experiences related to trauma or, in this case, to joy. It's akin to adding a drop of dye to a glass of water rather than pouring the whole bottle in at once. This allows the system to absorb and adapt to the change without becoming overwhelmed.

For someone dealing with joy aversion, titration might look like setting aside a few moments each day to engage in an activity that brings them a slight sense of happiness or satisfaction, such as listening to a piece of music, engaging in a brief mindfulness practice, or simply sitting in a park looking at dogs. The key is to start with very small doses of joy (you know, like tiny little joys?), allowing the person to gradually build tolerance and resilience to larger expressions of happiness over time.

We know that pendulation and titration are effective to treat trauma, so let's use them to treat the joy aversion that sometimes comes with trauma. We can think of them as gentle pathways that invite the nervous system to recalibrate and reopen to the experience of joy. By oscillating between comfort and slight discomfort (pendulation) and introducing joy in small, manageable doses (titration), we can learn to navigate emotional landscapes with greater ease and confidence. This process not only mitigates the fear and resistance associated with joy but also fosters a deeper, more sustainable connection to positive experiences, paving the way for healing and growth.

AVA'S BRIDGE

After Christina hung up on me, our relationship was finished, but my day was not. My next session was with Ava, an incredibly sweet and charming woman who was so freaked out by human contact that she couldn't handle the Zoom camera showing her whole face. She wanted to get to that point of comfort and felt it was important to challenge herself a little bit, so we adjusted to her fear. She tilted it up so that I could see just her eyes and her forehead. Ava's presence is remarkable, unique, and multifaceted. She is incredibly calm and serene, the kind of person you'd be glad you ended up stuck in an elevator with, and at the same time hilarious and irreverent. She is driven and accomplished, but she has giant, childlike eyes and a wild and creative imagination. One of her favorite things is fantasy fiction—she has these huge black bookshelves that line her living room wall and display hundreds of purple, gold, and silver book bindings with titles like *The Mists of Avalon* and *Dragonlance*. After our sessions, she would often take a concept we had talked about and create elaborate and fantastical drawings of it and then send them to me before our next session. Caves and dragons and rushing rivers featured prominently.

Ava's early years laid the foundation for a fortress around her heart. Experiencing trauma in childhood at the hands of foster parents, she learned to equate joy with vulnerability, and vulnerability with pain. Just like Christina. For Ava, moments of happiness were fleeting, only to be enveloped by the next wave of darkness. This instilled in her a white-hot fear of joy, which she likened to being cast adrift in a rushing river: uncontrolled, unpredictable, and potentially devastating. She preferred to be in her cave instead. As a result, her life was very small by design. She worked and came home and read her books, and that's about it. She had liked it that way. The world through Ava's eyes had become a landscape of hidden threats; her hypervigilance, her only shield. Joy was a siren's song, luring her toward the rocks of past injuries. She lived in the anticipation of the other shoe dropping, of joy being the harbinger of unforeseen pain. It was safer, she believed, to stand on the banks of life's river than to wade into its unpredictable currents. The only problem was that though she felt safe and protected in the cave, she was starting to want to poke her head out a little.

We started talking about the life she was living and how that differed from the life she wanted to live. She was stumped at first and then sent me a beautifully drawn picture of a dragon cowering and peering out of a cave. He was on one piece of land, and on his side everything was dark. There was a river, and on the other side of the river was another piece of land—lit up by the sun, full of wild-flowers, lush grass, and butterflies. "I'm the dragon," she wrote. "And I want to get to the other side. Desperately. But dragons can't swim—it's not even that I don't know how, it's that I can't and will never be able to—so how will I cross to the other side?"

I have to tell you: I am not a fantasy fan. It's just never appealed to me, and usually I roll my eyes any time dragons, butterflies—any of that shit—comes in. The last fantasy book I tried to read was in the fifth grade, and I threw it across the room. But Ava was so utterly charming and so clearly in love with fantasy that I suspended my disbelief. I'm so glad I did.

We start with the drawing at our next session. "I'm not going to be able to swim. I know you're going to say that you can teach me how to swim, but you can't. You can't teach me how to swim. I'll never get to the other side." Ava wants me to teach her how to swim but has built a barrier up to ensure that I won't. Our protective mechanisms are genius, but they spend so much time building their specific defenses up that they forget we can sometimes circumvent them entirely. The key is accepting them and figuring out a more creative way.

"I totally understand that. Dragons can't possibly swim. They are so heavy, and their wings aren't waterproof," I say. Accept the defense. Then find a creative way: "But, what if we just build a bridge?"

Ava blinks. She hadn't thought of this. "How do we do that?"

On the heels of my disaster with Christina, I have the same question.

With Christina's experience still fresh, I want to proceed slowly and make sure to have pendulation and titration in mind to prevent any snapback effect with Ava. On her lead, we start by building each of the worlds out. We start where Ava was already comfortable—in the cave. Over the course of a couple of sessions, we explore the cave together. What was it like in there? Comfortable. Dark. Solitary. "There's no one else's energy in here," Ava explains with her eyes closed. "I can take a deep breath." We learn a lot as we go. The cave had started being a theme for Ava because there was a giant chair in her foster parents' house that she used to turn into a fort. She could hide underneath it when she was scared or in trouble. No one else was small enough to crawl underneath with her, so she knew if she stayed under there, she was safe.

When Ava felt comfortable, we then started building planks away from fear and toward joy. Together we would brainstorm about small activities that she could do that pushed against her fear. One week she went and sat in a coffee shop and just watched people. The next week, she struck up a brief conversation with the barista. The following week, she asked an old friend to meet her for coffee. This one she was nervous about—she hadn't socialized outside of work in years and wasn't at all sure if she was going to be able to handle it. We decided that she could just make the plan and then see how she felt. We built her an out in case she realized she couldn't stay. As it turned out, she and the friend ended up sitting at the café for three hours, laughing and reminiscing about high school memories and gossiping about old crushes. When she came into her next session to tell me about it, her camera was tilted down, and I could see her whole face. I teared up as she shared her joy—fearlessly.

This essentially turned into a three-part epic that we embarked on together. You can do it too. It's fun and easy, and you can make it your own.

PART 1: CRAFTING THE WORLDS

The first thing to do is to understand where you are. Here, you'll visualize your "protective cave" and your desired "fantasy world." This will give you an unbiased idea of where you are, how you got there, and where you want to go. Remember, you don't have to do anything with it—yet.

> Step 1) Sit down and think about your protective cave—the place where you are protected from anything too overwhelming, including joy. You can write about it, draw or paint it, or both. As you do this, think about what makes it safe. What makes it confining? Include details about the environment, the feelings it evokes, and why you retreat here.

> Step 2) Now depict your fantasy world—the place you want to reach. You can do this on the other

side of the same sheet, or on another sheet. Let your imagination take over. What does it look like, feel like, smell like? Who or what is there with you? What activities bring you joy in this space? This is your place of uninhibited joy and fulfillment. Don't worry at all if there are aspects here that aren't real! They likely symbolize something.

Step 3) Reflect on what the river between these two worlds represents for you. Is it fear, past trauma, a belief system, all three? Or something else entirely? What happens when you step into that water? Write or draw these barriers, acknowledging what's keeping you from crossing to your fantasy world.

Step 4) If you are comfortable with this, share your drawings or writings with a trusted person. Discussing your protective cave and fantasy world can provide insight and make the next steps more tangible.

PART 2: BUILDING THE BRIDGE

Now that we're aware of what your cave looks like and why you've ended up there, as well as the world you want to get to, we need to think about how to move from one side to the other. Small, achievable steps are what we want here. And to always be aware that we can return to the safety of the cave as often as we need.

Step 1) Using the insights from Part 1, brainstorm potential "planks" or steps that could form a bridge to your fantasy world. These should be small, manageable actions or changes in thinking. For example, if the river represents fear of rejection, a plank might be reaching out to a friend for a chat.

Step 2) After completing your action, reflect on the experience. How did it feel? What did you learn? Take note of these steps and reflections to track your progress over time.

Step 3) Gradually add more planks to your bridge. Each should build on the previous ones, helping you to slowly but surely move toward your fantasy world. Celebrate each success, no matter how small.

PART 3: TAKING UP RESIDENCE

Now that we have started to titrate up to a more joyful life, it's time to solidify your place in your fantasy world. Don't worry, your cave is paid in full, and nobody can take it away from you! The goal here is to reverse the time spent so that you spend most of your time in your fantasy world and visit your cave when you need to rather than living in your cave and visiting the fantasy world.

Step 1) In your fantasy world, create a space where you feel most at peace and joyful. Capture this space somehow—find some pictures of what it might look like, draw something, or write down the details. Maybe it's a bench in a park, or a lovely little cottage on a hill. What does it look like? What are you doing there? How do you feel? This space symbolizes your ability to inhabit joy after months or years of inhibiting it.

Step 2) Commit to "visiting" this space regularly, through visualization, drawing, or writing. Each visit strengthens your belief in your right to joy and happiness. Recognize that the bridge you've built is not just a onetime pathway but a route you can travel whenever you need. You can visit your protective cave when necessary, but now you know the way back to joy.

Step 3) Celebrate your journey and, if you feel comfortable, share your experience with others. Your journey can inspire and encourage those who are also struggling to find their path to joy.

Ava's journey was not linear or free of setbacks, but that's what was so beautiful about the fantasy aspect of it—we set out for an epic journey, not a boring stroll. Also? We knew the scary bits were coming, and we had prepared for them. There were days when the river seemed too wide, the current too strong. But with each small act of bravery, each moment of joy embraced, she fortified her path across the river.

Ava gradually opened herself up to the broader spectrum of positive emotions—happiness, once a distant concept, became a familiar friend. She discovered that joy is not a harbinger of sorrow, and she now feels confident in feeling both, knowing that emotions are a tunnel, not a cave.

Your turn.

CHAPTER 6

Joy for When You Don't Believe in Joy

Hope is the thing with feathers.

—Emily Dickinson

TWO WEEKS AFTER I SIGNED THE CONTRACT TO WRITE this book, one of my closest friends was diagnosed with brain cancer. Stage 4 glioblastoma, a.k.a. *the really bad kind.* He's got twelve to eighteen months. *Max.* To add some more unspeakable awfulness to this story, he knows the road he's on all too well because his daughter Abi died of cancer at twenty-six. Selfishly, it felt a bit like the universe was taunting me. "Want to write about joy in the darkness?" it asks, laughing. "Here's some darkness. Go."

Why am I interrupting my own book to tell you this? Because I want to tell you that your relationship with joy might falter. In fact, you should expect that it will. There is no one-and-done fix where you welcome joy into your life and never doubt it again. Because in the middle of writing this book, I stopped believing in it and thought I might not be able to continue. But then I remembered that this book isn't just about joy, it's about joy in the darkness. And this is a story about how when writing this very book, I lost it and then found it again. Well, it found me. Right there in the dark.

They found out that Chris had brain cancer because he had a seizure. In the aura phase that comes right before a seizure, we were texting. I sent him a song I had just discovered and loved; he texted a Mary Oliver poem back and said, "Everything is related." Then everything changed.

For the first couple of weeks, Chris was immersed in a kind of postdiagnosis euphoria. He said that everything was suddenly clear and that he finally felt free. Fearless. He woke up from brain surgery smiling—no joke. He made friends with all the nurses and wrote about the beauty of the cancer ward. The first round of chemo and radiation was completed, Chris adopted a dog, and then shit got very real. Scan day came around again, and the cancer was still there. Chris was still dying, and the cancer ward was starting to feel a little stifling. He was trying to get to acceptance; his family and friends wanted him to keep fighting. He worried about whether he was dying well. What does that even mean to die well? "Better figure it out quickly," said the universe, tapping its watch.

Against this backdrop, the rest of the world feels quite

bleak. As I write this, the world is still grappling with the impacts of the COVID-19 pandemic; there are wars or ongoing conflicts across the globe; the gap between the rich and poor is widening in many countries, made worse by the economic fallout of the pandemic and leading to increased poverty and social unrest; rising global temperatures, extreme weather events, loss of biodiversity, deforestation, and pollution are causing irreversible damage to the planet (it's been raining in Northern California for more than two months); and many countries—most notably our own—are experiencing a rollback of civil liberties, with reports of censorship, suppression of dissent, and violations of human rights. And that's only a partial list. We're not in the '90s anymore, Toto.

Chris calls me one Tuesday afternoon and says urgently, "I can't feel joy anymore. Like, I know it's there? But a lot of it was tied up in things that I wanted to do, and my timeline is running out. What do you do when you can't feel joy anymore?" *What do you do when you can't feel joy anymore?* This is at once the very question I've been trying to ask and answer, and the question that leaves me slack-jawed and speechless. I have no idea.

I have more to tell Chris than I have time to tell it. I want to tell him about what the ancient Greeks said about dying well, and what Montaigne said about learning how to die. I want to make sure that he knows about quantum entanglement, and the fact that seven ounces go mysteriously missing when you die. But joy? Do we even have time for that? Do I have anything to say? What do you say about a thing you can't believe in?

I tell Chris that I can't feel it now either. Chris and I are friends largely because of shared losses. I lost my father and wrote about it, and he lost his daughter and wrote about it. It was like we had written want ads to the sky: "Fatherless daughter seeks replacement. Looking for the kind of person you can fall asleep talking to," and "Daughterless father looking for substitution. Must have irreverent sense of humor." As we waded through our grief, we shared the deepest and darkest parts. We did this gently, poetically. When trying to describe the kind of grief that knocks you over and has you clawing for the life exit, Chris came up with Virginia. Virginia (a.k.a. the kind of oppressive depression that makes you want to end your life) is like that weird aunt who comes to visit without announcing her arrival or indicating when she might be on her way. She just shows up at the front door with her musty, sofa-fabric-covered suitcases and stays for way too long. You open the door and groan. Somewhere on the third or fourth day, your dread turns to a kind of resigned acceptance. You didn't want her here, but she always brings those Oh Henry! candy bars. And she has some interesting family stories. She does the ironing. It's kind of nice to have family around.

Since I can't feel joy at the moment either, I tell him I recently found out that Virginia has brothers. The brothers are these two shadowy figures that came sloping into my house at some point, and I didn't even notice them. Maybe because they were dark and just sort of faded into the shadows? Or maybe I was just too tired or busy or distracted to fully see. They wait there in the shadows until I stand up from my desk, and before I can even get across the room or out the door, they are pushing, pushing. They put their huge hands on my shoulders and push down until I am silent and horizontal and frozen. Then they stand there and keep pushing. They cloud my brain and stop any momentum or forward movement. There is no rejection or rebellion or energy at all. They push and I stay. That would be fine, maybe, but then there is something I have to do. Some podcast I agreed to guest on. Some social media video I need to edit and post. Some session or meeting or appointment where I am expected to be a fully present human, not some haunted thing. And so the brothers stop pushing, and they pull. Pull me into the shower, into my clothes, into myself. And sometimes they prop me up because all their gravity hasn't let up yet. And then I stand up from my desk or walk into the living room and they slope out of the shadows, and it starts all over again. And I'm a haunted thing pretending to be a human, and you are dying, and I'm supposed to write about *joy*?

When I tell Chris about the brothers, he doesn't ask me if I am having some sort of episode or whether it might be time to seek out some psychiatric care. He just dives right in while I experience the deepest, most breathless dark.

"I don't know if I've ever met the brothers, but I may have, and maybe it's the same with them as it is with Virginia. Do they just weigh you down and then lift you up? Or is there more? How trustworthy, albeit unlikeable, might they be? What color are their eyes? Do they have hair like Shakey

Graves? Someone else? What language do they speak? Can you make out any of the words?"

It was like Chris stepped out of his email and into my living room with a flashlight exclaiming, "Boy, it's dark in here! Let's look at what kind of dark it is. What else is here?" Curiosity changed everything, as it always does. The brothers took shape; I noticed their black clothes, their shaggy hair, their kind blue eyes. The more I learned about them, the less frightening and oppressive they became. In their own way, they were here to help. I had been too overwhelmed for too long, and they were trying to get me to rest. So, I did. And then they left. They'll be back, and so will Virginia, because arriving unannounced runs in the family. But when they come, I know what they're here for and what to do.

I am telling you this story because I want to remind you of two very important things about hope and joy. The first is that you don't *have* to believe in them. And the second is that sometimes they show up dressed in sweatpants instead of sparkly tights, and if you don't know that, you might miss them.

BELIEF WHEN YOU DON'T BELIEVE

The word *belief* is just as rich and full of holiness as you might think. It means to have confidence in something— to hold something dear, to love it, even—without having demonstrated proof of it. Belief is irrational in a way. To believe is to commit yourself to something that you specifically do not know. It is a kind of transcendence. It's a miracle. It shows just how much of existence is not revealed to us, only intimated.

To be honest, I think belief takes itself a bit too seriously. You know how they tell you that if you run into a bear in the woods that you should make yourself all big and scary and intimidating so that when the bear weighs its fear against hunger, fear wins? Belief learned that trick, fooled a big scary bear, and now permanently stands tall, all raised arms and faux threat. My students ask me often if I believe in things—theories, countertheories, philosophies, and theologies. "Oh, I don't know what I believe. That's not really my job here," is how I always answer. They roll their eyes and throw their hands up in frustration. It isn't my job, but I'm also evading the question. I crawl away like the scared bear, licking my paws, still hungry.

This lack of belief—especially in difficult times when we need it the most—is an ache, an unquenched thirst, an unsated hunger. It leaves us crawling, desperate and fixated on our poor lot. All we can think about is the lack; all we can do is wish for it to be filled. There are some things we can choose to believe in or not, and then there are things that just are. And here's the miraculous thing about joy and hope: *you don't need to believe in them.* They will simply show up. All you have to do is leave just enough open space so that you notice them when they do.

I know, I can say that until the cows come home, and pigs fly, and I turn blue. But you, in all your lamenting lack, will resist unless I show you. I get it—I've been there too. Recently. So, I'll show you by turning to that same source I turned to on the first anniversary of my father's death, and nearly every deep, dark moment I've encountered since: very old books written by people who walked our very same path.

PROUST'S PETITE MADELEINE

There is a very famous passage in the first volume of *In Search of Lost Time* (also known as *Remembrance of Things Past*) by Marcel Proust, where he takes several pages to detail his experience of eating a petite madeleine cookie. This first volume is called *Swann's Way*, and you don't need to know a single thing about Proust or the book for this passage to pack a punch. I still vividly remember where I was the first time I read it.

It's an unremarkable winter day when Proust is visiting his mother and his fictional hometown, Combray. His mother notices that he is cold and offers him tea, and with it, one of those petite madeleine cookies—those French butter cookies that look like scalloped seashells. Proust dips the cookie into the lime-flower tea, puts it in his mouth, and bam.

No sooner had the warm liquid, and the crumbs with it, touched my palate, a shudder ran through my whole body, and I stopped, intent upon the extraordinary changes that were taking place. An exquisite pleasure had invaded my senses, but individual, detached, with no suggestion of its origin. And at once the vicissitudes of life had become indifferent to me, its disasters innocuous, its brevity illusory—this new sensation having had on me the effect which love has of filling me with a precious essence; or rather this essence was not in me, it was myself. I had ceased now to feel mediocre, accidental, mortal. Whence could it have come to me, this all-powerful joy? I was conscious that it was connected with the taste of tea and cake, but that it infinitely transcended those savours, could not, indeed, be of the same nature as theirs. Whence did it come? What did it signify? How could I seize upon and define it?[1]

That's one hell of a cookie.

Right before this passage, the narrator is lying in bed, unable to sleep and musing on the nature of insomnia, his annoyance at the elusiveness of sleep and a kind of frustrated wonder at where our minds wander in this state. If you've ever had even a single night's rest stolen by insomnia, you know exactly what the next day feels like—you find yourself all heavy lids and limbs, gauzy and disconnected. I picture Proust exhausted and foggy headed as he sits at the table— not jolly and exuberant.

And yet. It is in this diminished, fuzzy state that joy comes and finds him. It comes unbidden. It's so intense it stops him in his tracks; it's almost violent. He's not searching for joy or even anything adjacent to joy; he's simply trying to get warm. And this joy that finds him is not tiny; it is immense. He calls this joy "all-powerful," invoking God. It rights the crooked world. This joy is so powerful that it makes "disasters innocuous," makes his life feel important, meaningful, immortal rather than "mediocre, accidental, mortal."

When he's able to regain his bearings after being knocked over by this strong sensation, the narrator is able to trace it back to its origin—a joyful, sweet, and untouched memory of visiting a favorite aunt and being invited to share tea and madeleines with her. It's revealing that we spend so much time talking and writing about the traumatic memories that haunt us in a similarly intense and unbidden way, but we give almost no heed to the joyful ones that do. The moment when spring turns to summer and the smell of wet grass sends you careening back to summer camp, or you walk by an ice cream truck and get punched in the face by the memory of your favorite sweet treat, or someone on the internet posts a photo of a toy that you loved and forgot. The joy is right there, right next to the suffering, right next to the pain.

While this is the most vivid example of joy in *Swann's Way*, there are many similar moments that appear in subtle forms—through the beauty of nature, the pleasure of anticipation (such as waiting for his mother's good night kiss), and the comforts of familiar routines. These moments of joy are not restricted to positive experiences; they often coexist with or are directly followed by reflections on loss, change, and the achingly ephemeral nature of time. A part of what Proust is trying to reveal is that joy and sorrow are intertwined in the fabric of memory—precisely not because we choose to believe in them, but because this is simply how it is.

Sorrow doesn't need us to believe in it for it to exist, and we would all willingly admit as much. What we would be more skeptical of is the fact that the same is true for joy.

You don't need to believe in it. It will just show up and interrupt whatever you are doing, whatever is going on, and right the world. Just in case you're still skeptical, let's look at one more.

VIRGINIA WOOLF'S SUNBEAMS

Virginia Woolf's *To the Lighthouse* is more about disappointment than joy—although joy appears in the third sentence. It is a roaming, rambling tale that features enormous passages of stream-of-consciousness and relatively little by way of plot. The story follows the Ramsay family through a decade of vacation at their summerhouse in Scotland. In the first part of the novel, called The Window, we meet the family at their summer home. This is a vacation, and yet there is an immediate sense of tension and disappointment as a much-anticipated trip to the lighthouse gets canceled due to weather. Mrs. Ramsay thinks about having to break the news of the cancellation to her excited son, and it puts her in a state of melancholy. Almost as quickly as she is plunged into that melancholy, she plucks herself right out of it.

> Always, Mrs. Ramsay felt, one helped oneself out of solitude reluctantly by laying hold of some little odd or end, some sound, some sight. She listened, but it was all very still; cricket was over; the children were in their baths; there was only the sound of the sea. She stopped knitting; she held the long reddish-brown stocking dangling in her hands a moment. She saw the light again. With some irony in her interrogation, for when one woke at all, one's relations

changed, she looked at the steady light, the pitiless, the remorseless, which was so much her, yet so little her, which had her at its beck and call (she woke in the night and saw it bent across their bed, stroking the floor), but for all that she thought, watching it with fascination, hypnotised, as if it were stroking with its silver fingers some sealed vessel in her brain whose bursting would flood her with delight, she had known happiness, exquisite happiness, intense happiness, and it silvered the rough waves a little more brightly, as daylight faded, and the blue went out of the sea and it rolled in waves of pure lemon which curved and swelled and broke upon the beach and the ecstasy burst in her eyes and waves of pure delight raced over the floor of her mind and she felt, It is enough! It is enough![2]

In five sentences, Woolf pulls off a tremendous feat—anchoring the story, resolving the tension, and restoring hope. We go from darkness, disappointment, and melancholy to intense happiness, brightness, even ecstasy. "It is enough! It is enough!"

This is the passage that sparked the tiny little joys practice from Chapter 1 and set the foundation for *The Joy Reset* in the first place. In the summer of 2020, I was living in a temporary rental on the very top of a hill with two of the loudest and most chaotic housemates in all of creation. The research job I had been enjoying for the past year had lost funding, and suddenly I was without a steady paycheck and scrambling to stay afloat. My marriage was ending. I was three thousand miles away from almost everyone I knew and had lost a home to go back to. The pandemic was at its peak, everything was terrifying, and there was nowhere to go. Even the hiking trails by my house were temporarily closed. Oh, and California, the state I had just moved to, was literally *burning down*, and the power was out for three days at a time. I developed a habit of pacing around my little apartment listening to jazz standards recorded in the '30s and '40s on noise-canceling headphones.

Just about the only good thing at that moment was this amazing window right next to my bed that looked out onto the side of the hill. I was sitting there one morning sipping coffee and looking out at the horizon and the trees and remembered this passage from Virginia Woolf. Just as that sliver of light licking the waves over the floor of her mind shifted everything for Mrs. Ramsay, this passage shifted everything for me. It was like that moment when a camera comes into focus and suddenly everything in the viewfinder is crystal clear. Yes, we are living in a dark time. Yes, everything is awful and scary at the moment. Yes, I am lonely. These were big, huge, dark, and scary things. But they could not steal everything. There was this window. This light. This cup of coffee. This deep breath. None of these little things negated or erased the big bad things, but realizing they were still there in spite of the big bad things was an opening. That opening was a miracle. That opening was enough.

Unlike Proust, Mrs. Ramsay actually does go searching for something to anchor herself, to carry her out of the darkness. But she does not make the mistake that we do in assuming that it has to be something equally weighty to cancel out the darkness. She goes searching right away for something small, "some little odd or end."

Small things—the taste of a cookie that transports you back to childhood, the sight of a sneaky sunbeam, or the sound of a sweet song ringing out in the din—these are the game changers.

I know how hard it is to be struggling so much that you stop believing in goodness. But the great news—and this is proven in my life and yours and each of these stories and a thousand more—is that hope and joy don't give a shit if you believe in them. They are tenacious. Just as tenacious, if not more, than sorrow or fear. All you have to do is hold on and they will show up, looking for you. Even—especially—in the darkest moments.

What do you do when you can't feel joy? You just wait. That's it.

RECOGNIZING JOY

When we define joy and hope incorrectly, we make two critical mistakes. The first is that we don't understand them. We miss their complexity and power, their grit and irreverence. We sell them short. Just because these are considered positive emotions does not mean that they are one-dimensional. To bite Whitman a bit: Joy and hope contain multitudes.

Joy sometimes shows up as relief. These are tiny little mercies in your grief, depression, or anxiety. You know how you can only really sob for so long before your body needs something? After some amount of time you yawn, or take a big breath, or get hungry. Speaking of hunger, have you ever noticed how good that first meal after a couple of days of illness is? How wonderful it is to have the feeling of hunger again, and then to satisfy it? Or how you sometimes have a great night of sleep in the midst of a terrible time of grief, and wake up wiggling your toes with gratitude before you're even fully conscious?

Joy sometimes shows up as contentment. A Sunday afternoon where you get to spend an hour reading a novel on the couch, a morning walk in your familiar neighborhood, a gratifying ritual of catching up with a friend on a weeknight, finishing a crochet project, petting a cat, the smell of that grapefruit dish soap you love, the satisfaction of getting into a bed with fresh, clean sheets. This kind of contentment can feel so quotidian, so mundane, that we take it for granted, we don't really register it at all.

Joy sometimes shows up as acceptance. A conversation you have with your therapist where you finally see that you are not solely responsible for the demise of your marriage, that liberating feeling when you let go of your disappointment in the shitty spring weather and embrace a cozy day inside, the moment when you stop wishing that your parents could have been different and start to feel curious about how they got to be the way that they are.

And joy sometimes shows up indirectly—when we witness someone else's joy. For a year and a half, I spent a good chunk of hours in the Denver airport every other week. If you've never been there, the Denver airport is certainly somewhere in Dante's version of hell. I suspect it's in the ninth circle, but I might be biased. As I sat there one day, so steeped in misery I could have been mistaken for a Tim Burton character, I noticed this little girl in the terminal. She was about five and had red hair just like mine, and she was wearing a yellow tulle dress and twirling. Her arms were stretched out as she spun, and she was laughing at her dizziness. No one was interrupting her or trying to get her to stop or be quiet, and her delight was contagious. I started smiling and noticed that several other people in the terminal were noticing her too and also smiling. Delayed flights and airport misery be damned; joy was right here too.

There's actually a word for this, and it's as delightful as a little girl twirling in sunshine-colored tulle—*freudenfreude*. It comes from German and might remind you of its more commonly cited evil twin, schadenfreude. Schadenfreude is the joy that you feel at someone else's misfortune (like when you laugh hysterically because you've just seen someone fall down the stairs). Freudenfreude is the joy that you feel at someone else's joy.

Sometimes I wonder what the world would look like if we imprinted these lesser joys, these tiny mercies. What I do know is that when we do this individually, our worldview changes. To that end, here are a couple of fun tools to help you notice joy when joy is dressed up like some thirty-four-year-old video game addict who lives in his mother's basement.

MAKING YOUR SENSORY TREASURE MAP

You might have noticed in the examples from literature that in each example, one of the senses was the doorway to the experience of joy—Proust's tastebuds, Mrs. Ramsay's retinas. Our senses are powerful tools and even more powerful if we know what they like.

Grab a piece of paper. Imagine that it's not just any old paper; it is a treasure map where you will chart the hidden gems of your sensory world. If you're someone who navigates the world with a unique set of senses, embrace that! List only the treasures you can discover and enjoy.

Step 1) Imagine each of your senses as an island waiting to be explored. Dedicate a space on your paper for each sensory island, leaving open waters (three to four blank lines) between them. If an island is beyond your horizon, simply sail to the next; focus on the senses you are attuned to.

Step 2) Embark on a treasure hunt. Below each sensory island on your map, jot down the jewels you cherish the most (i.e., the things that most delight each of your senses). For the Isle of Aroma, maybe you'll find peppermint whirlpools, cinnamon caverns, almond groves, and lavender fields. On the Vista Viewpoint, you might look for glittering shores, sunset mountain majesties. Don't rush: this expedition might uncover sights, sounds, and sensations you've never paused to appreciate before. Keep your map with you, and whenever a new gem shines through the fog, chart it. (If anyone asks what you're writing, fuck 'em—this is for you.)

Step 3) With your map richly detailed, you stand at a crossroads.

Option 1) Display your map somewhere you can see it often—your command center (ahem, desk), your bathroom mirror, or your fridge. When the seas of life get stormy, glance at your map. Choose a few sensory gems to guide you back to calm waters.

Option 2) Assemble a portable treasure chest to take with you. Place small totems that remind

Isle of Aroma (Smell)

Vista Viewpoint (Sight)

Texture Bay (Touch)

Echo Cove (Sound)

Tastebud Terrace (Taste)

you of what you picked: photographs of breath-taking views, a vial of essential oil, a playlist of soul-stirring tunes.

Here's the thing: whether you do this exercise or not, these sensory joys will find you. But if we know that the senses offer a doorway into joy, why not leverage it? (So much of the best of life happens through the senses: food, music, sex, art.) By creating a sensory treasure map, you're actively recognizing and valuing these moments instead of just waiting for them, thereby rewiring your brain to seek and appreciate the beauty in the everyday. Remember the rewiring from Chapter 1? This is how we operationalize that.

In essence, this exercise is not just about *identifying* what brings you joy; it's about actively *incorporating* those joys into your daily life, making it a powerful tool for those struggling to feel joy in their everyday existence. Let it act as a beacon, guiding you back to presence, connection, and joy.

FREUDENFREUDE FIELD TRIP

This tool is my all-time favorite when I am low, low, low. It's inspired by my mother, Suzanne, who loved to do many things, but perhaps nothing as much as people watch. My mother looked like Grace Kelly and would have fit in better as the Princess of Monaco than she did a working mother of six in western Massachusetts. She had the kind of impeccable style that comes from being a keen observer. She was fascinated by people—what they wore, how they walked and gestured, whom they were with. Each person that walked

by offered up a whole universe of questions. When I lived in
New York and she would come visit for the day, 80 percent
of our time was spent perched on a bench in the park or in a
restaurant or in a café, just watching people.

It's a great way to engage with the world when you are
feeling drained or low energy because you don't have to
interact—just observe. Here I want you to look specifically
for joy on other people's faces, in their gestures and their
gait.

Step 1) Get yourself somewhere where there are
other people. Anywhere. It can be a park, a café, a
museum, a mall, whatever's nearby.

Step 2) Wait, and watch, and look for other people's
joy. Notice how it gets expressed. Is it in their facial
expression? Their animated gestures as they tell their
friend a funny story? Do their eyes get big? A smirk?
The way that they walk? Their bright clothes? Are
their dogs smiling?

Step 3) As you notice more and more joy, scan your
own body and emotional landscape. What kinds of
joy tend to be more contagious for you?

ACCIDENTAL GRACE

Chris called me this afternoon. I was in the middle of something, but without pause I got up from my desk and went to

sit on the windowsill because I know there are days coming where I will wish with all 10^{27} billion bouncing atoms in my body that I could just pick up the phone and talk to him.

Chris and I are running out of time, and we've got work to do. You only know which conversation is going to be the last in hindsight. So, I pick up the phone. "Hey!" I say, not waiting for a response. "Do you know about Proust's petite madeleine?"

PART 3

JOY

SHAME

CHAPTER 7

Joy Guilt

Each of us is more than the
worst thing we've ever done.

—Bryan Stevenson

REMEMBER FRANK? MORE THAN THREE YEARS AFTER his release, Frank's life is soaring like one of his doves. He's carefully carved out stability and normalcy in his life. He has a steady job, a new apartment far from his room overlooking skid row, and he has repaired some of the relationships that had frayed during his years of incarceration. And yet, as much as the outward signs point to success, something gnaws at Frank with every step he takes.

One morning, Frank calls me on his way to work. We don't have a session scheduled, and I haven't heard from him in two years, but I pick up the phone on the second ring. In between his questions about how I am doing, I can feel a tumultuous energy coming through the phone.

"Frank, don't get me wrong, I love hearing from you. But I'm getting the sense that you didn't just call for a catch-up." "MC, I've been feeling . . . wrong, somehow. Like I don't deserve any of this. The job, the apartment, even the air I'm breathing." His words tumble out, a torrent of confusion and guilt. "I keep thinking about the guys still inside, about the lives I can't bring back. And here I am, living. And not just living or surviving or whatever, but climbing. Thriving. I went into Whole Foods the other day for lunch, MC. Whole fucking Foods! It keeps getting better, and it feels like I'm betraying them, enjoying what they can't."

Here it is, another joy thief: a deep-rooted, misguided, but powerful guilt that is threatening to undermine the positive changes Frank has worked his absolute ass off to achieve. In Frank's case, it is a kind of guilt armed with an unanswerable question: Why do you get to be here, thriving, while the other guys lie in their graves or rot in jail? This guilt is more than just a shadow, it is a ghost that has its hands around Frank's neck, threatening to choke all the joy out of the new life he is building.

I know this kind of guilt well because it has not only plagued my clients, but it's also plagued me.

The weather on the day of my father's funeral was as cutting as the loss of him. It was December 28, and the air was all icy razor blades as we walked up the long sidewalk with his casket. My legs shook as we walked my father down the aisle—that same aisle that I had imagined him walking me down since I was a little girl. I stared at the maroon carpet and counted each step to ground myself until we got to the front of the church and our reserved first pew. I didn't lift my head up until we had sat down, and when I did, I came face to face with a life-size painted plastic camel standing about four feet away.

I had been attending St. Mary's parish since before I was born, and the place was full of holy memories. First communions and confirmations and my brother and I playing on the church steps while our parents stopped to chat. My favorite thing, though, was the nativity scene that was set up each year at Christmastime. The pieces were made of frosted glass, and they were delicately tucked into a little alcove on the side of the altar and lit up with museum lights. It was tiny and fragile and magical, and I loved to stand in front of it while the adults stood in line waiting for communion.

The year my father died, though, the church had decided to do something a little more . . . festive. Instead of the delicate glass nativity scene, they had gotten a life-size, full-color plastic nativity set, which was placed right in front of the altar. We had no idea until we sat down in front of it on the second saddest morning of our lives. The absurdity of sitting in front of an orange camel with red painted lips was made even more absurd by the fact that my dad thought that fake life-size animals—and especially talking animals—was the funniest thing on earth.

And so that's how I ended up laughing at my father's

funeral, hard enough that I started to worry I would be thrown out, and maybe committed. This laughter was such a sweet relief in the face of the past month of fast horror. But almost as soon as it started, a judgmental thought sliced through the merciful relief and whispered, "Are you seriously laughing at your father's funeral?" And just like that, the joy of the moment skittered away and was replaced with a gray and icy grief that took my breath away. We were supposed to wait at the back of the church for the processional, but instead we popped our black umbrellas open and walked straight to the limo. My mom looked like Grace Kelly escaping paparazzi. Time slouched. And joy didn't dare to come back for a long, long time.

So, here's the painful pattern, the aching little story arc: go through something terrible, hold on, force your way through the pain, get continuously knocked over by waves of grief, start to feel just a little bit better, and then boom. Get smushed by a ten-ton guilt anvil. Seriously? If hope and joy are so badass, why do they get so utterly and instantly bamboozled by guilt every goddamn time?

HOW GUILT BECAME A THIEF

We need to do a (quick) deep dive to understand how guilt gets in the way here. Let's first step back and think about emotions in general. We sometimes think of emotions as optional—a state of mind that we can either entertain or opt out of. "Oh, stop being so dramatic!" we might say to someone who is having an emotional reaction. Or "cool your jets," "calm down," "let it go." In each of these flippant and dismissive statements hides an insidious and misguided belief: if you are having an emotion that is inconvenient for you or anyone else, simply stop. As everyone who has ever been told to calm down knows (which is everyone), this does not work. Not one bit. Because emotions aren't optional states of mind that we can simply control however we please.

The truth is emotions are biological experiences that influence our behavior, decision-making, and social interactions. And each one of them—from the most lauded to the most publicly awkward—exists for a reason. In fact, from an evolutionary biology perspective, emotions are thought to serve a critical function in our survival. They enhance our ability to socialize, stay connected to others, and reproduce.

Just for a moment, throw out whatever you think about emotions (i.e., they are a sign of weakness, they are only for wimps and chicks, they are something that you should keep to yourself, etc.) and think of them instead as sophisticated biological mechanisms that have been honed over millennia to respond to the complexities of survival and reproductive success. Each one serves a purpose, guiding us toward beneficial outcomes and away from harmful ones. They help to motivate behaviors that are crucial for navigating social hierarchies, finding mates, avoiding predators, and securing resources. Not so wimpy now, eh?

Let's look at some examples of the purposes that emotions serve. Fear is probably the most straightforward emotion to understand from this perspective. It arises in response to perceived danger, preparing the body to effectively handle threats through the fight, flight, freeze response. In the case of fight or flight, the heightened state of arousal enables quicker reflexes, increased strength, and heightened senses—all of which are advantageous when facing predators or other dangers. In the case of freeze, the dampened state of the nervous system helps us hide from predators and feel less pain. For our ancestors, the quick identification and reaction to threats would have been crucial for survival, selecting for a strong fear response.

Think about love using the same framework. If you've ever been around a baby for more than, oh, twenty-five minutes, you know quite well that if we did not love our offspring, we would eat them. OK, maybe not eat them, but caring for them during their screaming and crying years would be a whole lot more difficult than it already is. The intense bond between a parent and their offspring ensures that the parent remains committed to providing for and protecting their young, at great personal sacrifice. Similarly, the bonds between mates (who, let's be honest, can also be super irritating) increase the likelihood of successful reproduction and the stability necessary for the prolonged care required by human infants.

Fear and love are pretty easy to situate here, but what about something like jealousy that does not seem to promote anything positive or survival based? The thinking goes like this: jealousy arises from the threat of losing valuable relationships or resources to rivals. Intense emotion—intense enough to often be described as something that eats us alive—can motivate behaviors aimed at ensuring the fidelity of a partner, thereby protecting one's genetic interests. In terms of resources, jealousy can motivate the defense of valuable assets necessary for survival and reproductive success. Though the results of jealousy are not always productive, the underlying motivation is to secure advantages for oneself and one's kin.

OK. But what about guilt?

The word *guilt* has its roots in the Old English word *gylt*, meaning "crime, sin, moral defect, failure of duty." Ouch. Here it seems to be related to having committed a specific offense rather than an amorphous feeling that someone can carry in regard to their general behavior or way of life (like Frank). Tracing it back a bit further, this Old English term is believed to come from Old Norse *gjald* meaning "debt, repayment; penalty, fine." This suggests an underlying concept of debt, something that is owed and needs to be paid back. In other words, guilt is what you feel when you do something that would offend others, and it is supposed to motivate you to repair, or pay it back in some way.

In ancestral environments, humans lived in relatively small, interdependent groups where cooperation was essential for survival. Sharing resources, providing mutual aid in times of sickness or injury, and collaborating in hunting and defense against predators were critical behaviors. Guilt served as an internal mechanism to enforce the social norms that made such cooperation possible. For example, when an individual failed to share resources, this could jeopardize the survival of the entire group. Guilt would prompt the individual to share more generously in the future, thus reinforcing the norm of sharing and contributing to the group's overall well-being. Similarly, an individual who did not contribute to group efforts, whether through laziness or hoarding resources, would likely experience guilt. This emotion would motivate them to act more cooperatively in the future, ensuring their continued acceptance within the group.

Clearly, then, guilt can be understood as an emotion that evolved to promote behaviors that are beneficial for group living and cooperation. We are much more likely to stay safe and alive when we are ensconced in a group rather than fighting for our lives individually. And collaboration can be tricky, especially when stakes are high. It might be tempting to lie, cheat, and steal our way to the resources that we need, but this is not a sustainable choice. As soon as people realize we are doing this, we will be ostracized and by extension, unsafe. Feelings of guilt help us stay in the group in two ways. They can help prevent us from doing things that would ostracize us because they arise any time we even think about acting against the social norms or expectations of the group. In cases where we have already taken the offending action, the feeling of guilt motivates us to rectify the situation, thus reinforcing social bonds and cooperative behavior.

In today's complex societies, the basic principles underlying the role of guilt remain largely the same, even though the specifics of how guilt operates have evolved alongside social complexity. In modern contexts, guilt maintains its role in reinforcing social bonds, like the ones between friends, family members, and romantic partners. When a person neglects or harms these relationships, guilt motivates actions to repair the damage—through apologies, increased attention, or other reparative behaviors. Guilt also functions within professional and communal settings to promote responsibility and accountability. For instance, if someone shirks their duties within a team, letting down colleagues, the resulting guilt can motivate them to fulfill their obligations more diligently in the future, maintaining harmony and productivity within the group.

On a broader scale, guilt can influence behavior related to social justice and environmental stewardship. Individuals may feel guilty for participating in or benefiting from systems that cause harm to others or the environment. This guilt can drive actions aimed at reducing one's negative impact, advocating for change, or contributing to causes that address these issues.

So, guilt serves as an internal regulatory mechanism that has evolved to promote behaviors conducive to social cohesion and cooperation. Here's what's so exciting about that: it means that neither I, nor Frank, nor you are doomed to be chased by joy guilt. If guilt serves a purpose, we just need to fulfill that purpose in order to get rid of it.

GIVING GUILT A GODDAMN JOB

Sometimes I wonder what kinds of conversations I might have with my clients—and what kinds of conversations they might have with each other—if we met in completely different circumstances. If Frank and I had been stuck on an elevator together, who would have spoken first? Would we have told our life stories, become friends, or maybe just silently nodded at each other, averted our eyes, and then waited? Most likely we would have sized each other up and decided that we could not possibly have anything in common before the elevator doors had even closed. But as it turns out, Frank and I have a lot in common. And there is one thing in particular that we all have in common. All of us are guilty of a set of transgressions of our own creation. Each and every one. But we cannot let this guilt steal our hard-earned gritty joy.

My first instinct when talking to Frank was to tell him that his guilt was simply wrong; it didn't belong. He had served his time, and he was doing so much good in the world, and the benefits he was reaping from his work were his to enjoy. The guilt he was feeling was a trick, and if he kept listening to it, it was going to slowly tear his life apart. When we don't believe that we deserve something, we sabotage it.

But contrary to what they tell you when you are preparing to take the SAT, your first instinct is not always right. Frank's feelings of guilt are not going to be assuaged by my telling him they don't belong. Saying that emotions are wrong is a little bit like when toddlers cover their face and tell you to come and find them because they don't think you can see them when they can't see you. Guilt will just giggle, think, "Oh, they're so adorable and really do not have a grip on reality yet," and continue to dog Frank. We need a better approach.

"Frank, what if you think of guilt almost like a herding dog?"
Frank laughs. "MC. *What?*"
"Herding dogs need a job, right? Otherwise, they will tear up the whole house. If you're going to have one, you had

better give it a job. Let's assume that your guilt is valid. It's here and it's in your house and right now, it's tearing up the house. Let's give it a job and see if it stops."
"Ohhhhhhh. I'm picking up what you're putting down. What kind of job?"

We already know that guilt is designed to serve a purpose. And it's here trying to get Frank's attention and make sure he fills that purpose. That purpose can't just be to "give up everything that brings you joy, because that's what you really deserve." We need to redirect the guilt, not by denying its presence or validity, but by understanding its underlying message and constructive potential. Just as a herding dog's instincts can be channeled into productive tasks, the energy of guilt can be redirected toward positive ends.

The first step here is turning to the guilt and finding out what it is trying to signal. In Frank's case, the guilt seems to be trying to highlight a discrepancy between the way he is living and his values—showing him that there is some way in which he is falling short. He feels that he walked away from a hard life and into one that is too easy. One where he shops at Whole Foods, a place he thought he'd never belong. So, what's the corrective action here? How can we use it as a catalyst for growth? Hint: it's not to stop shopping at Whole Foods.

Frank can bridge the gap between his life and values by thinking of ways he can use his current position in life to make amends or contribute to his community. Remember, the origin of the word has to do with repaying debts. We know that Frank already served his time, but this new debt seems to have arisen from life on the outside being easier than he expected. What else does he have that he could offer back to the world? He could offer his time to causes that align with his values, volunteer at a homeless shelter or food bank, mentor at-risk kids, coach a football team, work with other people who are trying to reintegrate into society just as he did. When we give guilt a job, it ceases to be a destructive force and becomes a constructive one, helping Frank to align his actions more closely with his ideals.

Maybe more important, this approach softens guilt because Frank will stop thinking of it as an enemy and more as an important mechanism of his moral compass. It invites a dialogue with our inner selves, one in which guilt becomes a teacher rather than a tyrant. Through this lens, we recognize that guilt's presence indicates not just where we've gone wrong or what we owe, but also where we aspire to improve and expand.

In embracing guilt in this way, we not only mitigate its capacity to cause emotional turmoil but also embrace the opportunity for personal development and social contribution. This reorientation toward guilt doesn't dismiss the emotion but gives it a constructive role, allowing us to find a path forward.

This same path can be taken if you're feeling guilt after grief. For me, that guilt didn't just come up on the day of my father's funeral, it came up every time I felt anything positive for several years after he died. This guilt serves a purpose too. One of the things we almost never talk about when we talk about grief (which we just don't talk about enough in general) is the way that joy can make you feel like you are losing all over again. Moving on can feel disloyal and bring an intense amount of guilt. But moving forward doesn't mean you're leaving your lost loved one behind. Emerson says that these are the moments in which we "court suffering";[1] we try to bring it close to us in the hopes that it will secure what we've lost, make real again what has slipped from reality. It doesn't work, though, he says, and I would add that it's simply not necessary. You can't leave your loved one behind, because they exist within you, and nothing can ever change that. It's the one mercy that comes with the finality of loss— the person you've lost becomes fixed within you. You cannot lose someone you've already lost.

Another thing we don't talk about enough when we talk about grief is that just because the person dies, does not mean your relationship does. This is a tricky concept, and I always hesitate a little when I bring it up with grieving clients because in the beginning stages of grief, all there is is lack— an enormous, ominous, taunting absence. I remember someone telling me three days after my dad died that I could still talk to him. I wanted to tell them to fuck right off because while everything else seemed a swirling and uncertain abyss, the one thing I did know was that he was never going to walk into the kitchen again, and we were never going to have another conversation. But I talk to my dad all the time now. And I know exactly what he would say.

Without knowing it at the time, I also tried to turn my

guilt into a herding dog. I gave it the enormous job of trying to live in a way that my dad would have been proud of. And to continue bringing as many of his qualities into the world as I can—kindness, acceptance, curiosity, humor. I'll never master these completely, but that's not the point. It is the continued trying that quiets the joy thief of guilt and allows me to experience the joy that is his memory.

REDIRECTING YOUR JOY GUILT

Listen, if joy guilt hasn't come for you yet—it will. It can be a significant barrier to embracing joy. And it's sneaky, so it might come from various places. It can hide in the stark contrast between past suffering and present success like it did with Frank, and it can hide behind inappropriate church laughter at your father's funeral. But joy and hope can fight back (and win) if we understand that guilt, like all emotions, has an evolutionary purpose and a message.

Step 1) The first, and maybe the hardest, step is to acknowledge that the guilt is there and turn to it without judgment. Start with the presupposition that it's a natural response and it has surfaced for a reason. Write down your feelings of guilt. Where are they coming from, and what are they telling you? Are they coming from grief and telling you that you are betraying someone by moving on? Are they coming from success and telling you that you don't deserve what you've got? No matter how ugly

Redirecting Joy Guilt

THE GUILT I'M STRUGGLING WITH:

_____

_____

_____

_____

_____

_____

IDEAS TO REDIRECT THAT GUILT TOWARD SOMETHING POSITIVE:

_____

_____

_____

_____

_____

_____

THE REDIRECTION RITUAL I AM COMMITTING TO:

_____

_____

_____

_____

_____

_____

the message, get it down on paper. Take a deep breath. Writing it doesn't mean agreeing with it.

Step 2) Now that you understand what your guilt is communicating, it's time to redirect it toward something positive. Imagine that your guilt is a debt that has to be repaid, and write down how you can pay it back. This involves finding actions that align with the message guilt is trying to send, but in a constructive way. So, if guilt stems from thriving after hardship, consider how you can use your current position to help others who are where you once were. If it's about moving on from a loss, think about ways to honor the memory of the loved one while still allowing yourself to seek happiness.

Step 3) Now create a ritual or commitment. This is how you keep the joy guilt from coming back over and over again. This could be volunteering, mentoring, starting a project that reflects your values, or establishing a ritual that honors a lost loved one while still affirming life. The key is to transform the energy of guilt into actions that feel meaningful and aligned with your values.

Step 4) Gradually allow yourself to embrace the joy that will come from redirecting the guilt. Go back to the tiny little joys exercise from Chapter 1 (page 26), and do it specifically with this. What are the TLJs you find in your ritual? This is a double whammy—turning guilt into its own kind of joy is just the kind of subversive trick that joy is made for.

The more you do this, the more you will start to see joy guilt not as an obstacle but as an opportunity for deeper understanding and a new kind of joy. It's about honoring where you've been while giving yourself permission to move forward. This process isn't about eradicating guilt but about integrating it into a larger narrative of healing, growth, and renewal.

You might be wondering about me and my own joy guilt. Guilt chased the joy away on the morning of my dad's funeral, and joy stayed gone for a long time. If my dad had still been alive, he would have laughed right along with me at his own funeral. Unabashed. He would have let us all get thrown out of mass, and we would have laughed all the way out and doubled over in the parking lot. I don't really remember my dad's laugh, exactly, but I remember that it was irrepressible.

I write my dad a letter every year on Christmas—which is the anniversary of his death. The word "letter" is sort of a misnomer because these letters feel more like conversations than missives. I tell him how I'm doing, what's new, what the past year has been like. I ask him questions, tell him all the things that I wish we could talk about, thank him for the lessons that he taught me.

When I tell him that I'm working too much and it's starting to eat me alive:

"Oh, Mac. You do such nice work. Go put your feet up and eat some Cheetos!"

When I detail the incredible drama I encountered this last year in academia:

"I have always thought that those guys were bullies. The whole system is designed to cut people down. You are so much more than that. What a shame. I am so disappointed in them."

When I tell him I'm writing a book about joy:

"Oh, I'm so pleased! Over the weekend, I googled 'joy terms' and came up with this list. We can talk about it in the car on the way home from New Haven."

When I tell him about a speaking gig I get to do at a pretty huge conference:

"Oh! I can't wait to hear about it when you get home!!!"

When I got into graduate school the first time, which was just a year before he died, he wrote me this email:

Hey Mac,

I can't tell you how happy I am for you!!! What great news!!!! Bask in the glory, delight in the prospects, feel the energy of what is to be discovered and created and what you love to do. You are on the way. Have a great evening of celebration. I'm so proud of you—you put yourself out there—shoot for the sky—accept the decisions with grace—and march into the sunset whatever happens.

Love Dad

And for my twenty-fourth birthday, just a few months before he died, he wrote me this at 4:54 a.m.:

Hey Mac,

HAPPY BIRTHDAY TO YOU—HAPPY BIRTHDAY TO YOU—HAPPY BIRTHDAY TOOO YOOOOU— can you just hear me singing this. Maybe it's better that you can't. At least you will be able to read this in your very own apartment! Hope your day will be perfect—tell everyone not to bug you today—tomorrow maybe but not today.

Love Dad

Maybe we can tack Dad's advice onto the joy-guilt exercise. The next time joy guilt shows up unbidden, you can tell it that Bob said not to bug you today—tomorrow maybe, but not today.

CHAPTER 8

Joy Shame

> When you soak a child in shame, they
> cannot develop the neurological pathways
> that carry thoughts of self-worth.
>
> **—Hannah Gadsby**

YOU'VE PROBABLY HEARD THAT THE DIFFERENCE
between guilt and shame is that guilt leads you to think,
"I did a bad thing," or "I made a mistake," whereas shame
leads you to the much more damning and definitive conclu-
sion, "I am bad," or "I am a mistake." That's a great con-
ceptual definition, but it's not visceral enough. And shame is
visceral. Shame isn't just the bigger, scarier older brother of
guilt. Shame is guilt metastasized. The psychological equiva-
lent of a localized cancer that has reached your liver and gets
carried through your blood to every other organ and system

in your body. Guilt is treatable. Shame is terminal. That is, unless we intervene, and quickly.

You wouldn't know that Sarah struggled with shame if you met her. Her life certainly doesn't indicate it either. She's an incredibly stylish knockout with a successful career in finance, a gorgeous artist husband, and three Gap model–worthy kids. She's whip smart and witty, and so emotionally attuned that I *almost* don't notice when she steers the conversation away from her and back to me. If I'm not careful, we'll spend a whole session *not* talking about what she came in to talk about—which is the fact that though her life is Instagram worthy from the outside, inside, the wheels are coming off. Her shame cancer is manifesting in two particularly destructive symptoms: secrecy and rage.

First, the secrets. Sarah is married to the love of her life, Ethan. He's handsome and a successful artist, which is nearly an oxymoron. They've been together for fifteen years, and even with all that time and three children, there's still a spark. She lights up when she talks about him, like a sixteen-year-old in love for the first time, and I imagine he does the same. And yet. Seemingly inexplicably, Sarah has started an intoxicating, disastrous affair with a coworker—an investment analyst named Brad, who she thought was a total dirtbag when she met him. She *still* kind of thinks he's a dirtbag; she just can't stop sleeping with him.

Sarah—attuned, engaged Sarah—can't hold eye contact when she talks about it.

"When I met Brad, I was actually repulsed. Completely, entirely repulsed. I hated him. He's so arrogant, so dark, so . . . You know, the first time we had sex, we were in the middle of a huge argument about an earnings forecast report. It was like a scene in a movie. All that anger just somehow transformed into sexual energy—I always thought that trope was total bullshit. Ugh. I *hate* him. I don't get it." She glances at me for a millisecond and then looks away. The thing that strikes me the most in her narrative is that she does not hold even one ounce of compassion for herself. It's pure battery acid self-hatred all the way down.

And don't get me wrong, what Sarah is doing is not OK. She knows that, and I know that, and she knows that I know that. We are both aware of the ethics and the urgency here. This one awful secret has the potential to tear apart Sarah's whole life. Her job, her marriage, her relationship with her kids. And she doesn't even *like* the guy.

And then there is the rage. Somehow at the same time as this has been going on, she tapped into a simmering rage that had bubbled under her life unnoticed for years. Maybe decades. She's enraged at her family for the difficult way she had to grow up, her husband for his idyllic childhood, her friends for not being able to understand her, and her children for being so 24/7 needy. This rage is *way* out of character and makes Sarah feel even worse about herself. Further compounding it is that the guilt about the affair she is entangled in and can't seem to stop has lodged itself under her skin and impacts every second she spends with her family. She is hyperaware of every mistake she makes as a parent, no matter how small, and is consumed by the fear that she is damaging her children. This fear has led to increased anxiety, which manifests as irritability and impatience with her children.

> "I slammed the door in Liam's face last night. He's only three. He was crying about bedtime, and I so desperately needed to get in the shower just so I could *think*, you know? And he was so needy and so grabby, and I just snapped. God. I'm a terrible mother."
>
> She puts her head in her hands, flooded with another wave of blazing self-loathing.
>
> "Oh, Sarah, you're not a terrible mother. You're *really* overwhelmed. Listen, I know you're doing things that you don't want to be doing right now. I know you know it's wrong, but the thing we have to figure out is how to stop it. I think to get there, we need to understand *why* you're doing this in the first place. These behaviors—which are behaviors you're engaged with and are not who you are, by the way—are not in line with your values. They are symptoms of a deeper disease. Let's unpack some of this."

SHAME: A PACK OF THIEVES

It occurs to me as I'm working with Sarah that shame might be not actually its own distinct thief, but something that can come into existence only when all of them band together. Like that final level in *Super Mario* where you have to fight all three of the bosses at the same time, and it's so impossible that you can't believe *anyone* has ever won the game without cheating.

Sarah grew up in a trailer park. Her mom was an addict who split when she was just a toddler. Nobody knew where her mom had ended up, and Sarah got the impression that they were kind of afraid to go searching for fear of what they might find. Her dad was a tragic figure—a sad and stricken functional alcoholic who loved Sarah to pieces and tried *so goddamn hard* to make a better life for her. Tried but couldn't quite get it together. Couldn't quite stop drinking. Never got them out of that trailer park. And it would be impossible to explain this to him because there was not an *ounce* of maliciousness in it at all, but he leaned on Sarah way, *way* too much. She was like his little wife by the time she was ten, cleaning and cooking and taking care of his emotions. And he used her intelligence, capability, and beauty as proof of his own worth. He'd march her around like a pageant queen, tell everyone how smart she was. "Did you see my little Sarah-bird?" he'd ask anyone they encountered. "She just learned how to make lasagna. She's only eleven. Can you believe it? And she is so good at math! Math, of all things! What, oh what, am I going to do if little bird flies from my nest?" Sarah hated the attention, but didn't know why. Her dad didn't either. He was complimenting her, or so he thought. But Sarah knew that none of her classmates lived a life like they did. That she was being held up like a little trophy. And that little girls aren't supposed to take care of their dads.

By the time Sarah was thirteen or so, she had already realized that if she wasn't careful to get out, and soon, she'd end up stuck in that trailer playing wife to her dad for the rest of her life. Or worse, she'd end up like her mom—with a story so ugly no one even cared to know how it ended. So, she put her head down, worked as hard as she could, and scored a scholarship to a big fancy school in Chicago— about as far away from that trailer park as she could get. She immersed herself in a sparkling finance career and just kept going, until she found herself inexplicably hitting the detonate button on her pretty little life. *Why?*

"Our firm just had our annual leadership summit," Sarah is explaining during a session. "I got a fucking *award*. I'm standing at this podium holding this stupid trophy like it's a Grammy or something, trying to give this stupid speech, and Brad is sitting there in the first row and he's fucking *winking* at me and it's *gross*, and I swear to God, I almost just admitted it all then and there. I just wanted to pop the bubble and say, I don't deserve this award. I don't deserve anything I've gotten. I'm just a disgusting trailer-trash slut, and I've fooled you all, and I'm fucking exhausted so here is your stupid award, I'm out."

This little daydream all soaked with disgust feels really relevant, so I ask Sarah if we can dive in there, even though I know she intended this to be sort of a throwaway story—just another way into the same question: What the fuck is wrong with me, and why am I hitting the detonate button on my pretty little life?

So, we dig in. Though Sarah talks about herself in unkind ways all the time, the derogatory names feel really specific this time, so I ask where they came from and what they mean to her (aside from the obvious).

> "Oh, I guess I never told you this, but I was bullied pretty badly in high school, and that's what they always called me. I got a lot of attention from the boys, and although I basically never took the bait, the girls just *really* hated me. It actually got violent, and the principal got involved. My dad cried in her office, it was so embarrassing, and of course none of that helped. I was Daddy's little bird at home, and at school I was a trailer-trash slut. I couldn't get away from it; it was awful."
>
> "No, you never told me that. Hang on, this is starting to make some sense . . ."

I explain to Sarah what I can suddenly see in her story—she has been trapped by two opposing identities—neither of which was of her own volition or creation. And yes, she got out, made her own life for herself—but now that life stands in opposition to those two identities—and so her system is trying to resolve the tension. This is why she's facilitating her own sabotage. She's trying to rip the Band-Aid off a wound she doesn't even have yet.

I wish we wouldn't dismiss the things that we went through in high school. It's such a critical developmental stage, and so much foundation gets laid down because of the events and relationships we have during that time. If Sarah had never been called a slut, and some stranger on the street called her one as she walked by, she would wave it off and move on with her day. Maybe laugh. But when children (and developmentally speaking, we are children until we are eighteen) hear the same negative labels or insults repeatedly, it shapes their understanding of themselves. Words like *slut* carry *heavy* moral and social judgments about a person's value, particularly related to their sexuality. If this message is repeated, children begin to believe that the external judgments reflect something *inherently* true about who they are. Even if they disagree with the judgment, the seed is planted anyway—the seed that their worth is tied to their sexuality or perceived sexual behavior.

Also, words like *slut* carry a sense of disgust and contempt. This also gets internalized—as it clearly has with Sarah. This emotional weight makes the insult feel not just like a label but like a core truth. This disgusting thing is *what you are.* The belief became part of her emotional fabric, rooted in feelings of shame, fear, and worthlessness.

When negative messages about a person's identity go unchallenged or unsupported by alternative, positive narratives, they take hold more deeply. If no one steps in to offer a different perspective or help the person process the emotional harm, the negative belief becomes their internal narrative. In this case, no one reassured Sarah that her worth is not tied to her sexual behavior or appearance—in fact, her father accidentally strengthened it. "She couldn't possibly be a slut," he cried in the principal's office, "she's my little bird!" Translation: she's not *that* kind of object that exists purely for other people's pleasure, she's *this* kind of object that exists purely for this other kind of pleasure.

Sarah thought she got away. And in many ways, she did. She got away from the trailer park and her father and her mother's unfinished story. But she did not escape her own shame.

In Sarah's case, since she was bullied with sexually derogatory terms, this led to internalizing the belief that she is inherently "slutty" or "bad." Her affair with Brad—who also disgusts her—is almost a way of fulfilling that prophecy, even though the behavior is driven by shame and emotional pain rather than desire. This creates a cycle of self-sabotage, where the internalized belief compels her to act in ways that reinforce the very shame she's trying to escape.

What about the rage? Sarah's rage isn't just random; it's an extension of the shame that's haunted her since childhood, and in true joy-thief fashion, it is shielding her from embracing the life she's built. This rage works like armor, allowing her to keep her deepest shame and vulnerability at a distance, ensuring she can't fully enjoy the life she's created for herself. On some level, Sarah still feels she doesn't deserve the success, stability, and family she has now. Rage, then, becomes a way of rejecting it before it can reject her—an emotional defense inherited from years of feeling inferior and unworthy. She may not consciously realize it, but by keeping herself detached from the good she has achieved, she's reinforcing the narrative that she's still that girl from the trailer park who isn't "good enough" for the life she's living now.

The affair with Brad also feeds this self-justifying rage. It's easier to feel justified in cheating when anger toward her family simmers below the surface, providing the perfect excuse for her actions. The resentment she feels toward her husband, her children, and even her idyllic life plays directly into her shame narrative. That rage isn't just for the here and now; it's rooted in her past, directed at the people who shaped her—at her mother, for abandoning her, and at her father, for being so helpless and needy, for leaning on her as if she were his equal, or worse, his substitute wife. This anger kept her going in survival mode, driving her to "get out" and leave that life behind. But it's also held her hostage, creating a cycle where rage justifies her actions and allows her shame to flourish unchecked.

Since she didn't integrate these internalized stories about herself, she recreated them in a different form. At home, she was the perfect wife everyone expected her to be—but internally raging against the expectations that had been laid at her feet since she was a child. Expectations that she could certainly fulfill, but no one had ever asked her if she *wanted* to. And at work, with Brad, she was a slut everyone expected her to be—having a torrid affair with the last person you'd imagine.

"Your actions don't just make sense, Sarah; it's almost a perfect duplication of the unresolved dynamic."
"Whoa. Wow. I can totally see it."
"It's the work of the joy thieves! They banded together and merged each of their individual voices until they became one, relentlessly chanting in your ear, 'you *do not* deserve *this*!' And what do you do when you find yourself in a situation that you don't deserve to be in? You find the red

button and you smash it. Hit detonate. Sabotage. When we look at it that way, your affair is not just a random act of infidelity. It's a manifestation of the joy thieves. They've metastasized into something bigger, something worse. They've morphed into shame."

Though she didn't grow up in a gang like Frank, she was just as hypervigilant—poised and ready for any eventuality. Like Christina, she learned to anticipate the worst, always bracing herself for the next blow, whether it came or not. When the blows did come, she learned to hide her emotions, because they only made things worse. Similar to Richie, she became emotionally numb because there wasn't any room for her own emotions when she was so busy taking care of her father's.

Sarah also knows that if her affair is discovered, she will lose everything she loves. That's not what she wants, but it's what she is sure is going to happen. It's what she's going to make happen. This particular affair suits her worldview of unworthiness. It's as if she's trying to prove to herself that she's unworthy of the love and success she's achieved, echoing the internalized messages of her childhood. The affair, repulsive as it is to her, shores up the joy thieves and serves as a twisted form of validation for the shame she's carried all her life.

As we work through all this, Sarah is relieved to figure out that there are reasons underneath her behavior. Reasons that make sense. She's also encouraged at the thought that once we banish the joy thieves, she'll be able to welcome hope and joy back in. The only question is, How? How do we do this?

Before we get into the doing, there's one thing we need to understand. If we set aside the judgment about what Sarah is doing, we can see that her behavior—influenced by the joy thieves turned systemic shame—is aimed at adaptation. These adaptive moves turned maladaptive over time, but the fact that she adapted in the first place shows that she is *adaptive*. We all are. Look at that hope sitting right there in the desperation. The brain that learned to shut down emotions and to keep joy secret and soak the whole system in shame is *malleable*. All we need to do once we recognize that an adaptation has become maladaptive is to readapt. This is within our reach. We *can* rewire our brain, we *can* forgive ourselves for what we reached for in desperation, and we *can* relearn how to welcome joy back in.

Rewiring the brain involves creating new neural pathways that promote feelings of safety, connection, and joy. As we do this, it is crucial to create environments where positive experiences are consistent and untainted by fear or shame. This involves not only individual efforts but also supportive relationships and communities that foster safety and acceptance. By cultivating these environments and intentionally practicing joy, we can help our brains rewire and rediscover the capacity for happiness.

REWIRING YOUR BRAIN

Imagine your brain as a super fancy computer, but instead of circuits and wires, it's made up of millions of tiny connections called neurons. These neurons talk to each other through electrical signals and chemicals, kind of like sending messages on social media. When you learn something new or practice something repeatedly, these connections get stronger and more efficient. This is called neuroplasticity, which is just a fancy word for the brain's ability to rewire itself.

For Sarah, shame became a deeply entrenched neural pathway, reinforced by the trauma of her childhood, the bullying she faced in high school, and her need to escape her upbringing. Her brain, wired for survival, used shame as a protective mechanism. It told her, "If I hit detonate on my life, no one else can do it first," and that created a vicious cycle of self-sabotage. The good news is that Sarah's brain—and any brain—can change. Just as it learned to associate her self-worth with shame, it can learn new associations with safety, connection, and joy. But rewiring the brain, like rewiring any computer, takes time, patience, and deliberate effort.

Now, let's talk about fear and how it can be extinguished. Picture this: You have a pet hamster named Hammy. One day, you accidentally drop a book loudly right next to Hammy's cage, and he gets super scared. After that, every time Hammy sees a book, he freaks out. Aww. Poor Hammy! The book has become a neutral stimulus that Hammy now associates with fear. But don't worry, all is not lost, and Hammy doesn't need to drown in his own pathology. Hammy's brain can be rewired to change this response.

To help Hammy, you start showing him the book from a distance while giving him his favorite treats, like tiny hamster cookies. Over time, Hammy starts to realize that the book isn't so scary when it comes with yummy treats. Slowly, you bring the book closer and closer, still giving treats. Eventually, Hammy's fear of the book fades away because his brain has rewired itself to associate the book with positive experiences instead of fear. This process is called "extinction," where the brain learns to let go of the old, scary connection and form a new, positive one. The same process applies to Sarah's shame. Every time Sarah faces an old trigger (like public recognition or being vulnerable with her partner) and chooses a new, positive response, she is rewiring her brain. The more she does this, the weaker the old shame pathways become, and the stronger the new, healthy pathways grow.

It seems simple because it kind of is. Your brain can rewire itself through repeated experiences, making strong new connections and weakening old, unhelpful ones. And just like Hammy, we can overcome fears and change our reactions by creating new, positive associations. The goal for Sarah is not to erase her past or pretend it never happened but to teach her brain that she is safe, that vulnerability can lead to connection, and that joy is something she deserves—not something to be feared.

SCALING DOWN THE SCARY

Shame teaches us that we should hide. That we don't deserve the things we earn in our life, and we should never let our vulnerability be seen because it will lead to rejection or worse—ridicule. Because vulnerability makes us feel so raw, so exposed, so, well, vulnerable, learning how to express ourselves can feel like an impossible task. For Sarah, the fear of being exposed—as a fraud, a failure, or a slut—was paralyzing. But to rewire her brain, she didn't have to leap into radical transparency immediately. That would have been too overwhelming and dysregulating for her nervous system. So, what's the answer? Scale down. This will feel familiar to you now because we encountered it in Chapter 1—scale way, *way* down to become accustomed to the new emotion without dysregulating the nervous system.

Step 1) Identify the fear. Start by identifying something that you've been hiding from because you're way too afraid to do it. It could be sharing an emotional experience with someone, telling someone a secret, public speaking, asking a stranger for help. Anything that you're ashamed of, that makes you feel insecure, or even something that you're excited about but afraid of being judged for. With Sarah, we identified that she was terrified of truly being seen by Ethan and her children. If she showed them her authentic self, she was afraid they would reject her. So, she tried to be perfect and kept secrets.

Step 2) Scale it WAY down. Scale the thing down. Way down. Think about what a "tiny" version might look like. For example:

Small Share: Maybe you're afraid of sharing your feelings about your relationship with your partner.

Instead of revealing *all* your feelings about your relationship, start by sharing a small thing, like something you appreciated that they did. Sarah started with small gestures—telling Ethan something she appreciated about him but had never said out loud. With her kids, Sarah gave up trying to be the perfect, all-knowing mom and started asking for their help in small ways and letting them see her make a mistake without rushing to fix it.

Tiny Gesture: Maybe you're afraid of expressing affection. Start with something small, like giving a genuine compliment to a stranger, or sharing a lighthearted memory with a friend.

Simple Question: Maybe you're afraid that if you don't know something, people will think you are dumb, so you don't ask questions. Instead of asking a question in the middle of a huge work meeting, walk into a shop and ask a stranger what time it is.

Step 3) Reflect and adjust. After each small act of vulnerability, take a moment to reflect on how it felt. Did it feel as scary as you imagined? What was the other person's response? How did you feel after they responded? Use this reflection to adjust your approach. If something felt too overwhelming, scale it down even further. If it felt manageable, consider taking a slightly bigger step next time.

After each small step, Sarah reflected on how it felt. Was it as scary as she had imagined? Did Ethan or the kids react negatively, as she feared, or were they receptive and appreciative? By reflecting, Sarah started to see that her fear of vulnerability was often exaggerated. The world didn't fall apart when she let her guard down a little. This reflection helped her brain learn that it's safe to be seen, little by little.

As she grew more comfortable, she was able to scale up her vulnerability—sharing more of her feelings, engaging in deeper conversations, and letting herself be emotionally present in moments she once avoided.

Vulnerability doesn't have to be all or nothing. By scaling down the scary into small, manageable steps, you can gradually get used to sharing your deepest emotions with those you love. Over time, what once felt terrifying can become a natural and rewarding part of your relationships.

GOLD STARS

Understanding the science behind fear conditioning and the developing brain provides a framework for why trauma has such a lasting impact and why the process of reclaiming joy requires deliberate and compassionate effort. It reminds us that healing is not just about overcoming fear but about actively nurturing and reawakening the parts of ourselves capable of experiencing joy.

Imprinting the negative stuff is automatic; the unlearning

process we have to do manually. And by rote. That doesn't sound fun, but I promise you it is. Plus, I'm going to give you gold stars.

Step 1) Order some gold-star stickers, or a metallic gold pen that you can make gold stars with. Really better if you can get the stickers, though. Go on. I'll wait.

Step 2) Identify a negative stimulus. Let's not swing for the fences on the first pitch here, though, so don't pick the worst thing you can possibly think of. Pick something that's slightly negative to start. This could be a task you don't enjoy, a part of your day that you find boring, or a situation that makes you mildly uncomfortable (doing that stretching routine, folding the laundry, eating a veggie you kind of hate but is a superfood because of course it is).

Step 3) Set a positive reinforcer. This could be a small treat, a fun activity, or just simply that gold-star sticker. Hammy had those hamster cookies; you pick something positive you will give yourself every single time you engage with the negative stimulus from Step 2. You're going to introduce the positive reinforcement whenever you engage with the negative stimulus. Be specific! "Every time I fold the laundry, I'm going to set a timer and scroll through TikTok for ten minutes." Or "Every time I have to do a

GOLD STARS!

Date:	Thing I don't want to do:	Action I took anyway:	Reward!
5/24/25	Exercise	20 minute dance party in the kitchen	Watching my favorite show

presentation at work, I'm going to buy myself a choc-olate bar to enjoy right after."

Step 4) Track your progress! Create a super simple chart on a piece of paper that has four columns— one for the date, one for the negative stimulus, one for the action you took, and one for the reward. At the end of a month, write a short reflection on how your feelings toward the stimulus have changed. Do you feel less negative or more neutral/positive about it now? You might notice, for example, that at the beginning of the month you had a ton of dread about the presentations you knew you had coming up at work. At the end of the month, you might notice that you have markedly less dread and almost find yourself looking forward to the presen-tations because you know you'll get a treat and a gold star.

You can do this with anything—from mundane tasks to much bigger and scarier emotional tasks. And I know it sounds simple and a little silly, but it works.

SARAH'S PATH FORWARD

I know that you will wonder about how the affair ended and what happened to Sarah. The details are irrelevant, but the affair ended. She came clean to Ethan, who was completely shocked, and they went straight to therapy to sort every-thing out. He moved out for a little while, as they slowly, painstakingly sifted through Sarah's past, examining each joy thief as they went.

Once they sorted through Ethan's anger, he was able to offer her the compassion and understanding that she never received from her parents and could not extend to herself. She is learning to validate her own experiences and trust that she is worthy of love and joy. Sarah is well on her way to healing the wounds that have driven her to keep secrets and to sabotage her own happiness. And she is aware that she needs to keep shame in check. She's in remission now, but shame can come back.

Unchecked shame is the ultimate thief of joy—it is guilt metastasized. It is a pack of thieves united into one, giant thief that will taunt you and trick you into thinking you are unworthy. Unchecked shame is terminal. But it doesn't have to be. We can banish it by shining a light on it, by bringing our vulnerabilities out of the shadows, and by rewiring our brains to know, without a shadow of doubt, that we are worthy of joy.

And, hey, whatever they called you in high school?

It was *never* true.

Epilogue

In the depth of winter, I finally learned that
within me there lay an invincible summer.

—Albert Camus

CHRIS CALLS ME THE OTHER DAY FROM THE BEACH. WE'RE almost at month twelve. He still has brain cancer—he will never not have brain cancer—but he had a good scan day recently. "It looks like we might get a little more time," he says, and I actually double over with relief. "But I'm so sick of cancer talk. Tell me about you. How's the book going?"

I tell him that it's dark. He pauses for a minute and asks if I set out to write a dark book about joy. He means it earnestly, but I laugh. I tell him I wanted to write a book about *real* joy, not bullshit joy. I set out to write a book for those of us who have been so banged around by life that we don't believe in joy, or think that it's a luxury we can't afford, or a thing we don't deserve considering the mistakes we've made. I wanted to show my readers the light that I've found in the dark, the joy in the sadness.

I know myself and I've seen in my clients that joy can be something we actively avoid. We avoid it because our hypervigilance tricks us into thinking we must stay on alert for threat, and joy forces our guards down. We avoid it because we are trying to numb our sadness or our anxiety, and we accidentally drown out joy. We avoid it because we are white-knuckle terrified of loss, and we have been shown exactly what we can lose and how fast. We avoid it because we've been conditioned to be afraid of it. And we avoid it because it makes us feel guilty. How could we indulge in this silly little emotion when so much is wrong with us, with the world, with both?

The story I usually tell is that I came to these experiences and questions about joy because of loss. My parents both died quickly before I was twenty-five. That's a clean story, and it's a true story. It happened and it blew my life apart. But it's not the whole story. There's a much deeper and more personal reason that I wrote this book and what I set out to do in it. To explain that, I have to start over with where I started, which is to say I have to start with my mother. She has been dead for sixteen years, and I still sometimes wake up with her corpse lying on top of me, and her bony hands around my neck. When she left, she bled all over me and then laid her haunted body on mine. "Finish this work," she croaked. "I couldn't."

My mother was the sun. We orbited her—one husband,

six children. Each our own isolated planet, flung through space and time by her gravitational pull. She was warm and loving and made everything possible, but if you flew too close, if you left your prescribed orbit, she would incinerate you.

No. My mother was the whole solar system. She was the sun and the planets. The hydrogen, the helium, the rock, the metal. She was the gravitational pull and the collapse that started time. The moons and the seas set their watches to her mood—there was only reacting to her, nothing fathomable outside of her.

No. My mother was a dark star. An object whose existence owes itself only to the darkness that surrounds it—its presence inferred by the eclipsing of other stars. She had a gravitational pull strong enough to swallow the light. She was a star heated—fueled—by annihilation.

No. My mother was a supernova. She was a dying, massive star. She burned nuclear fuel at the core, and for her whole existence was caught in between two opposing forces—gravity and pressure.

Stars are impossible objects. Light bursting in the dark. Stars exist because of forces outside of themselves. Stars are created out of nothing but tension, of contradiction. Stars burn nuclear fuel at their cores, which generates pressure. That pressure is what keeps the star from collapse. It pushes out against gravity and in return, gravity squeezes back. When the star runs out of fuel, the pressure pushing out drops, and gravity wins. The collapse happens so quickly and with such intensity that it creates shock waves that move from the center of the star and cause the outer part of the star to explode.

When a massive star reaches the most chaotic point of star death (yes, this moment can be measured), it creates a supernova, which is an explosion that scatters heavy elements like gold and silver throughout the universe.

If a star is big enough, it leaves a black hole behind when it explodes. A dense spot where gravity is so strong that nothing—no light, no atom, no wave—can escape. This is what losing my mother felt like. A loss that rendered the universe black and dense. Trapped. Her death stopped us orbiting, swallowed gravity.

My mother was a supernova and when she died, she scattered heavy metals throughout my universe. Gold, silver, lead. That may sound hopeful, but it's more complicated than that. Heavy metals cannot be created or destroyed. They are generative. Foundational. They are the components of Earth's crust. But in the wrong place, they are also toxic, destructive. It's my job to find them and sort them out. If I don't? That toxicity will win. So will gravity. My little star will explode.

"Finish this work," she croaked. "I couldn't."

"What work?" The dead leave us with unanswered questions. Nobody talks about that. A question is a strange thing to be haunted by.

My mother died sixteen years ago, and I only realized when I was writing this book that the work she left had to do with the joy thieves. This is partly because of the muddy grief that left me shocked and choking on her death, and partly because what she left behind is a multigenerational mess—a tangled root system that absorbs only darkness, fear, violence, and addiction from the soil and feeds it directly to the family tree. These roots tangle and tear, and the fruit we bear is so booze-soaked it splashes when it falls from the tree, rotten and sweet.

I found myself gagging on muddy grief not just because she died, but because the reason she died shattered every structure I had ever known. My mother—the terrible force that set the universe in motion—couldn't live without my father. That might sound like a small thing, but it destroyed my universe. Sent it orbiting in the opposite direction. Rewrote and rewired everything. I had been terrified of my mother since I was born, and it turned out that she wasn't something to fear—she *was* fear. When my father died, her facade crumbled. She couldn't live without him. She didn't live without him. We still needed her. I was twenty-five.

Grief isn't just about sadness. It's also about figuring out what a loss means—tracing its edges, discovering what it signifies, encountering just which of your structures of meaning have turned to sand. My mother's death and the circumstances that surrounded it meant that she was more wizard behind the curtain than she was the great Oz. It meant that I had formed an orbit around something that was suddenly revealed to be smoke and mirrors. It meant that nothing made sense. And so, when she died, I went careening into the sky—untethered and in mortal danger.

About a year after my mother died, I was in my therapist's office talking about why I struggled with weekends. Fridays had started to feel like the top of a roller coaster, plunging me into a dark and sticky two-day hellscape that I was never sure I would survive. As an afterthought, I laughed and told her about how many Saturdays were ruined in my childhood by my mom trashing my room.

"Wait. She what?" she said, then paused. "That's not funny."

It *was* kind of funny though. It was like my mom was doing a Tommy Lee impression, trashing a room at the Chateau Marmont. She would pull all the clothes from the closet, tip the bookshelves, break the things that I loved—things my dad had given me or even made for me. As soon as the hurricane winds started, I would start cleaning up after her. Diligently going through my belongings before she was even done tearing them apart, quickly stashing things that hadn't gotten broken, rearranging books and placing them quietly back onto the shelves. That must be it. I must have put them on the shelves in the wrong order. If I did it right this time, it wouldn't happen again. I liked them color coded. Let's try alphabetical.

Before she left, she would get in my face: "I am not going to let a little shit like you take me down." I wasn't sure how a child would even go about taking down a grown woman, but it seemed pretty dire.

Sometimes when I'm around my friends' kids, all their rosy-cheeked innocence hits like a sucker punch right to the gut and leaves me breathless. I know that all parents lose their shit every now and then, but treating a child the way that I was treated so regularly feels unfathomable.

There is a picture of me one year at Thanksgiving, age nine. We are posing for the yearly family photo, and I look frozen, haunted—like maybe I am being held by al-Qaeda and am desperately trying to get a message across with my eyes while keeping some approximation of a smile plastered on my face. I look stunned, like a bird that has flown into a window. Did I mention I'm nine?

Right before we shot the picture, my mother had yanked me by my arm into a hidden corner of the foyer and attempted to smooth down my unruly hair. I had been told to pick out my own clothes that morning, and I put on my favorite outfit: a pair of purple leggings and a purple shirt with a false vest and tie sewn on top of it, which gave the outfit sort of a rumpled, '90s-Prince purple-tuxedo look. Perfect. I pulled my hair into a ponytail, which I then decorated with a festive—and matching—purple bow. Right before marching me back into the living room, my mother bent down to face level, three inches from my pale face, and hissed: "Why do you always look like shit?" Each word a complete sentence propelled by contempt. Each word hit my cheeks like a tiny thumbtack bullet.

My therapist is right. I guess that's *not* funny.

The thing was, part of me is still stuck there in the foyer with my mother, trying to figure out what to say to the question, "Why do you always look like shit?" I didn't know why. I knew enough not to answer and that the question was rhetorical (although I doubt I knew that word yet). I didn't know what made someone look like shit or pulled together, stylish and elegant like my mother always was. How were you supposed to know? Were you supposed to pick the things that you liked to look at? Or should it be more about how they feel? I liked bright colors and soft fabrics and outfits that had good memories. So that's what I picked. That morning, I somehow picked wrong. I wore that outfit on my birthday that year, and it wasn't wrong then. That was only a month ago—what made it go to shit so fast? I didn't know why. I did know enough not to ever ask. Asking anything with my mother was asking for it.

"What did you do after?" my therapist asked.

"What do you mean?"

"What happened when these tantrums were over? Did anyone help you?"

I could tell that my therapist was stunned. That what I was describing to her did not square with her understanding of me as a baby adult. That she wasn't just asking what I did in the moment, but how I got out. How I ended up here in her office as I did—sunny, productive, optimistic, full of hope and ambition and a metric ton of fear but very little anger. Absolutely no simmering rage. I felt proud at her disbelief. "I didn't end up like her. Whew."

I really wish the whole story was that my dad saved me from my mother. And in so many ways, he did. On the day I was born, he stretched out his arms and held up the sky like a tent—making sure there was always a space where I was protected from her gravitational pull.

The rest of the story, though, is that I saved myself. With joy. A gritty, steely kind of joy that I found in the wake of my mother's collapsed star. And that impossible joy has been the thing that has saved me every single time I have been plunged into the suffocating dark. I had to write this book because I saved myself from my house and my mother by hoarding joy and hope like candy. I stashed joy away under my bedroom floorboards. I threw myself into my studies, chased independence, and kept secrets. I gathered experiences and relationships and found strength in the connections I made with others, people who showed me there was more to life than fear and chaos. And I am still practicing. Still fumbling and making mistakes and losing faith in joy and hope altogether and then laughing when they find me again, right here in the dark. But far more important than the story of me saving myself is what I learned while I was doing it, and I want to share that with you so you can save yourself, too.

What I learned writing this book was the answer to the question, "What work?" The work that my mother couldn't finish was this: manage fear, or *you will become it*.

Here's what makes it so hard to write about my mother: if you didn't know her, these stories make her sound like a monster. She wasn't a monster. She was terrified. Traumatized. Hypervigilant. She was terrified and doing the very best that she could, which was a whole hell of a lot more than she got. There were six pieces of her walking around outside of her and in danger. In danger of their own mistakes. In danger of encountering the world and getting swept up. In danger of soaking up everything that was in the roots of our family tree—darkness, fear, violence, addiction. In danger of breaking her heart. Fear like that slips through the cracks in the front door and fills the house like mustard gas.

Fear like that swallows everything. She could not keep her fear in check, and it turned into a simmering rage that she could not always control. Fear had her by the throat and she was exhausted, and so she became it. The thieves won.

One of the last conversations I had with her was an argument. As you can perhaps imagine, she was not a human that you would choose to tussle with if you could avoid it. It was a Friday afternoon; I had driven home from New York after work, and she had been officially diagnosed with metastatic colon cancer that day. It was in her liver, which meant it was everywhere. She had been desperately sick for half a year but had refused to go to the doctor. She thought it was grief that was making her lose so much weight so fast that her skin was dripping off of her body like a clock in a Dalí painting. I didn't know she would get a diagnosis that day, and so I stared in shock for a moment and then started to cry. And she raged.

"How dare you," she hissed from across the kitchen, pointing at me.

"This is happening to *me*, not *you*." She grew ten feet taller with each word. I was twenty-five, then fourteen, then six, then three. My father had just died. My mother was dying. *And still fucking yelling at me.*

"It is also happening to me," I roared back at her. I walked out of the room and up the stairs and then sat in the stairway and cried as quietly as I could, wondering if *I* was the monster. I remember this as if it were seven seconds ago. Nobody followed me. I stared out the window in the stairway. Winter sun sliced the street in half. The trees were beautiful. I loved this house and this little town. Crying felt cleansing. Relief. I took deep breaths.

It's been sixteen years, and I finally understand what she was really saying: "The thieves are winning. I've been fighting it for my whole life. Please help." If I had understood this then, maybe I could have saved her. Not from her cancer, but from the joy thieves.

I'm so sorry, Mom.

Maybe she left me this work because she thought I could finish it. Because she knew that I had hidden joy from her like stolen candy. Because she wanted me to teach you how, too.

So, go on then. Let's step out of this cave and march into the sunset.

Don't you see how it sparkles here in the near dark?

Acknowledgments

I always thought that the acknowledgments section was where writers get to give thanks and pay off debts. "Thank you for supporting me, and I'm making sure to put your name here with this little inside joke as recompense for the fact that this book has been a third party in our relationship for the past three years and hasn't even come out yet. Cheers!" This is true, but it's only part of the truth, because to acknowledge is to confess or admit what you *know*. So here is a thing that I know: this project would not have been remotely possible without the people listed here.

Renee Sedliar, you believed in this book before I did, and somehow shepherded us through at least two world crises and the one personal one where I thought we should just bail on the whole thing. You are a spectacular and steadfast guide, thank you. Laura Yorke, after the last *molasses disaster* of an adventure we had in this wild and wonderful world of publishing, I was pretty ready to be done. Thank you for encouraging me and staying with me despite my boundless pessimism.

Thank you to Old Dominion University for systematically stamping out nearly every ounce of love I once had for academia and belief I had in justice. From those ruins comes this light. And thank you to the College of the Holy Cross and my fabulous summer-session students for reviving that love yet again. I can't wait to see who you become.

Thank you to my clients, who show up with the most vulnerable and tender parts of their lives and trust me with them, again and again. You are clear-eyed, determined, and brave, and I am so proud of you.

Thank you to everyone at Hachette who has been involved in this project: Andrew Goldberg, Cisca Schreefel, Nzinga Temu, Nana Twumasi, Brynn Warriner, Sarahmay Wilkinson, Laura Gonzales, and Nan Rittenhouse. You all have been wonderful to work with. Let's do this again sometime, yeah?

To my friends: I walk around a little bowled over by wonder that we get to be alive at the same time and humbled that you choose me to be your friend. Jen, our "happy lists" from high school were a critical part of my becoming, and the fact that we have remained friends since the second grade is one of my proudest accomplishments. Thirty-five years, and I'm still jealous of your Coca-Cola bathing suit. Commander Jess T. Hill, you are an indefatigable joy, and the trust tree is and always will be one of my favorite places on this earth. Evan, there's a field somewhere, yada yada, I'll meet you there. Megan, your joy and enthusiasm have been a buoy in a wide and terrifying sea. Tracy, you are magic personified, and I am so lucky to have met you. Steph, you are an irrepressible flashlight of a human being, and I don't think you have any idea how bright your light shines. Jeanelle, your beautiful artistic soul restores my faith in humanity. Also, you have the best laugh. Chris, my life changed forever when you came into it. There is an infinite beach somewhere, and we will always be walking it with Bindi, having the deepest conversations and then pausing to laugh about something completely stupid. Lisa, thank you for being my first reader and my first phone call. We're going to celebrate this one, dammit. And Mark, you are not my friend (and yes, I will die on that hill), but you are the truest and most steady rebel I know. I have such admiration for the way you are in the world. Also, you're like, six hundred times cooler than me, but you don't seem to know it, and I really hope you don't realize it anytime soon.

Notes

Chapter 1

1. Robert A. Emmons and Michael E. McCullough, "Counting Blessings Versus Burdens: An Experimental Investigation of Gratitude and Subjective Well-Being in Daily Life," *Journal of Personality and Social Psychology* 84, no. 2 (February 2003): 377–389.

2. Katelyn N. G. Long, Eric S. Kim, Ying Chen, Matthew F. Wilson, Everett L. Worthington Jr., and Tyler J. VanderWeele, "The Role of Hope in Subsequent Health and Well-Being for Older Adults: An Outcome-Wide Longitudinal Approach," *Global Epidemiology* 2 (2020).

Chapter 2

1. Dacher Keltner, *Awe: The New Science of Everyday Wonder and How It Can Transform Your Life* (New York: Penguin, 2023).

2. Keltner, *Awe.*

3. "Homeboy Industries Thought for the Day April 26, 2021: Robert—Behold, Stand in Awe and Be Amazed," Homeboy Industries, April 28, 2021, YouTube video, www.youtube.com/watch?v=elAZTVQm2so.

Chapter 3

1. Albert Camus, *The Myth of Sisyphus* (New York: Vintage Books, 2018).

2. Nina Bull, *The Attitude Theory of Emotion* (New York: Johnson Reprint, 1968).

Chapter 5

1. David J. Morris, *The Evil Hours: A Biography of Post-Traumatic Stress Disorder* (Boston: Houghton Mifflin Harcourt, 2015).

Chapter 6

1. Marcel Proust, *In Search of Lost Time*, trans. C. K. Scott Moncrieff and Terence Kilmartin, rev. D. J. Enright, vol. 1, *Swann's Way* (New York: Random House, 1992), 60–62.

2. Virginia Woolf, *To the Lighthouse* (New York: Harcourt, Brace, 1927), 99–100.

Chapter 7

1. Ralph Waldo Emerson, *Ralph Waldo Emerson: Essays and Lectures*, ed. Joel Porte (New York: Library of America, 1983), 472.

Index

absence, 94
absurdity, 68–69, 72, 76
abyss, 4, 9, 72–78, 81–82, 86, 89
acceptance, joy as, 159
accountability, promoted by
    guilt, 177
adaptation
    to anxiety, 129–130, 132
    automatic, 105
    to hypervigilance, 132
    imprinting, 12
    to stress, 132
    thought of suicide, 70
adaptive response, 118–119
affair, shame from, 190,
    197–199, 208
allostasis, 128–130, 135
amygdala, 13, 14, 101–102
Anderson, Jamie, 107
anxiety
    adaptation to, 129–130, 132
    awake to, 87
    emotional numbing, 16
    hope circuit, 103–104
    postpartum, 123–124
    reduced by gratitude, 6
    snapback, 130
    tiny little mercies in, 158
associative learning, 13
audit, quick hope and joy, 24–25

Ava (client), 136–144
aversion, joy, 131, 133–136
avoidance
    illusion of control, 125
    joy, 212
    pattern of, 14
    vulnerability, 132
awe
    fighting hypervigilance with,
        56–60
    as joy for an experience, 88
    resetting default mode
        network, 54
    sources, 55–56
    transformation, 89
    ubiquity, 55–56

behavior
    adaptive, 118–119 (see also
        adaptation)
    cooperative, 176
    default, 118
    emotions, influence of, 173
    guilt, influence of, 175–177
    maladaptive, 200
    ours as baffling, 39
belief when you don't believe,
    150–152
big ideas, 55
Boyle, Greg, 33, 59

brain
  default mode network, 39–48,
    50, 52, 54, 56
  hope circuit, 2
  malleability, 13
  neural circuits, 40,
    100–102, 200
  neuroimaging, 7–9, 41
  rewiring, 163, 200–202, 209
  structures, 41–44
bridge, Ava's, 136–144
Brown, Brené, 113
Brown, Jerry, 34–35
Bull, Nina, 88

Camus, Albert, 67–73, 76, 211
career, 85
cave, protective, 137–144
CF (cystic fibrosis), 95–96
Chris (friend), 146–150,
    164–165, 211
Christina (client), 1, 3–5, 15, 19,
    23, 113–114, 120–126, 132,
    136, 139
circuits, neural, 40, 100–102,
    200
clients, author's
  Ava, 136–144
  Christina, 1, 3–5, 15, 19, 23,
    113–114, 120–126, 132,
    139, 146
  Frank, 33–38, 46–52, 54–55,
    58, 169–170, 177–180
  Lena, 19–23
  Richie, 61–68, 73–75, 77,
    80–81, 89
  Sarah, 190–205, 208–209
collective movement, 55
compost pile, 25–26, 28

conditioning, 17, 119. *See also* fear
    conditioning
contempt, 124–125
contentment, joy as, 159
control panel, resetting your
    values, 84–86
cookie, madeleine, 152–153
cooperation, reinforced by guilt,
    175–177
cortisol, 131
COVID-19 pandemic, 2, 147, 157
crisis, existential, 77–81, 100
curiosity, 80, 150
cystic fibrosis (CF), 95–96

danger
  labeling joy as, 125–126
  prioritized lessons of, 13
  response to, 10–11, 102, 173
  triggers, 120
darkness
  abyss, 72–77
  Camus, 68
  fear of, 66
  finding your way in the dark,
    77–81
  preparing for, 78
  steps when plunged into, 81–89
daydreaming, 42, 127
death, and grief, 180–182,
    214–215
debt, guilt as, 175, 179–180, 184
default mode network (DMN),
    39–48
  "baseline/resting state" of the
    brain, 41
  brain structures, 41–44
  discovery, 41
  influencing, 44, 47

memory, 45
negativity, 39–40, 44–46,
   52, 54
resetting, 46–48, 50, 54, 56
responsibilities, 40
shaking up, 52
TV analogy, 41, 45
depression
oppressive, 148
reduced by gratitude, 6
simmering, 125
tiny little mercies in, 158
Dickinson, Emily, 145
DMN. *See* default mode network
dopamine, 13, 103, 131

Emerson, Ralph Waldo, 94, 181
emotional numbing, 61–89
description, 16–17
protective mechanism, 66
Richie (client), 61–68, 73–75,
   77, 80–81, 89
emotional suicide, 67
emotions
as non-optional, 172–173
purposes served by, 173–177
simmering, 125
endorphins, 131
environmental stewardship,
   influence of guilt on, 177
envy, 125
epinephrine, 131
essence, 68–69
existential crisis, 77–81, 100
existentialism, 68–73, 75–76, 79
extinction, 202

fantasy world, bridge to, 138–144
fawn (trauma response), 10–11

fear
author's mother's, 219–220
emotional numbing, 66
extinguishing, 201–202
inhibition by hope, 102
of joy, 125, 136–137
of loss, 17, 93–111
purposes served by, 173–174
scaling down the scary,
   202–205
simmering, 125
fear circuit, 101–103, 105
fear conditioning, 113–144
adaptive response, 118–119
associative learning, 13
joy fear, 17
mapping the developing brain,
   role in, 13–14
science behind, 205
snapback effect, 126–132
triggers, 118
felt sense, 108–109
fight, flight, freeze response, 10–12,
   114, 116, 131, 173–174
Floyd, George, 2
fMRI (functional magnetic
   resonance imaging), 8–9
Frank (client), 33–38, 46–52,
   54–55, 58, 169–170, 177–180
freedom, and existentialism,
   70–72, 77
free writing, 24–25
freudenfreude, 160
freudenfreude field trip, 163–164
functional magnetic resonance
   imaging (fMRI), 8–9

GABA (gamma-aminobutyric
   acid), 130

Gadsby, Hannah, 189
gangs, 34–35, 37, 47, 59
gold stars, 205–208
gratitude
    imprinting, 6, 108
    mainstay of psychological
        health, 6
    studies supporting effects
        of, 7–9
    supercharged, 109–110
    tiny gratitude acts, 107–109
gratitude lists, 107–110
gratitude practice, 8
grief
    death and, 180–182, 214–215
    guilt after, 180–182
    joy within, 106
    tiny little mercies in, 158
growth
    catalyst for, 179
    integrating guilt into narrative
        of, 185
    pendulation and titration, 136
    personal, 7, 84–85
    posttraumatic, 4
guilt
    affair-related, 191
    giving a job to, 177–182
    joy, 169–187
    joy shame, 18
    origins of term, 175
    purposes served by, 175–177,
        180, 182
    redirecting, 182–185
    shame difference from, 189–190

happiness, distrust of, 121, 123
Hawthorne, Nathaniel, 61
health, 85

heavy metals, 214
hippocampus, 11, 13, 43
Homeboy Industries, 58–59
homeostasis, 128–131
hope
    audit, quick, 24–25
    fear inhibited by, 102
    mainstay of psychological
        health, 6
    opposition triggered by, 15
    rebellious, 93, 100
    studies supporting effects
        of, 7–9
    as tenacious, 158
hope circuit, 100–107
    activating, 2–3
    author's use of, 4
    kindness to others, 105–106
    snapshot of, 2
hormones, triggered by joy, 131
hunger, 158–159
hypervigilance, 33–60
    adaptation to, 132
    default mode network, 39–52
    description, 15–16
    fighting with awe, 56–60
    Frank (client), 33–38, 46–52,
        54–55, 58
    as shield, 137
    snapback effect, 131–132

imprinting
    adaptation, 12
    gratitude, 6, 108
    negative experiences, 13,
        44, 205
    tiny little joys, 23, 26, 28, 160
In Search of Lost Time
    (Proust), 152

insomnia, 153
Into the Wild, 79
In Treatment (HBO show),
132–133
introspection, 40, 42

jealousy, 174–175
Jeremy (friend), 93–97, 99–100,
104–107, 111
joy
audit, quick, 24–25
avoidance, 212
as danger, 125–126
fear of, 125, 136–137
freudenfreude field trip,
163–164
within grief, 106
incorporating into daily
life, 163
intentionally practicing, 200
labeling as danger, 125–126
opposition to, 15
recognizing, 158–160
rejection of, 127
saved by, 218–219
scaling down, 25–29
sensory, 160–163
snapback effect, 131
stolen by trauma, 9–19
stress reduced by, 131–132
as tenacious, 158
titration, 135–136
as trigger, 114, 120–126
as verb, 98–99
for when you don't believe in
joy, 145–165
joy aversion, 131, 133–136
joy fear, 17, 125, 136–137
joy guilt, 169–187, 212

author's, 170–172, 185–187
Frank (client), 169–170,
177–180
how guilt became a thief,
172–177
redirecting, 182–185
joy resistance
emotional numbing, 16–17,
61–89
hypervigilance, 15–16, 33–60
joy shame, 189–209. *See also*
shame
description, 18–19
guilt, 18
joy thieves, 15–19, 29, 198–200,
214, 221

kindness, 6, 105, 108

lateral temporal cortex (LTC), 43
learning, associative, 13
Lena (client), 19–23
Levine, Peter, 133
life, encountering the beginning
and the end of, 55–56
limbic system, 101
loss, fear of, 17
love
purposes served by, 174
transformation of, 107
LTC (lateral temporal cortex), 43

madeleine cookies, 152–153
maladaptive behavior, 200
McCandless, Chris, 79
meaning
relabeling your files, 83
searching for, 82
that we give life, 69

meaninglessness, 68–69, 72,
74, 76
meaning making, 76–77, 82, 89
medial prefrontal cortex
(mPFC), 42
memory
default mode network, 45
hippocampus role in, 11, 14, 43
joyous, 154
pendulation, 134
trauma, 133–144, 154
triggered, 115–117
mercies, tiny, 158, 160
mindfulness, 52
mind wandering, 40
moral beauty, of others, 55
music, 55
The Myth of Sisyphus (Camus),
57–68, 72–73

nature, 55
negative emotions, suppression
of, 66
negative experiences
default mode network, 44–45
imprinting, 13, 44, 205
prioritizing, 13–14
negative stimulus, 206, 208
negativity, default mode network
and, 39–40, 44–46, 52, 54
neural circuits, 40, 100–102, 200
neuroimaging, 7–9, 41
neurons, 100, 201
neuroplasticity, 201
neuroscience, 7–8, 100, 104–105
neurotransmitter, 13, 102–103,
130–131
Newton's cradle, 133
numbing. *See* emotional numbing

panic attack, 63, 129–130
parasympathetic nervous system,
131–132
Pavlov, Ivan, 119
PCC (posterior cingulate
cortex), 42
pendulation, 133–136, 139
personal growth, 7, 84–85
petite madeleine cookies, 152–153
positive psychology
evidence-based therapeutic
interventions, 6–7
research supporting, 5–9
positive reinforcement, 206
positivity, toxic, 29
posterior cingulate cortex
(PCC), 42
postpartum anxiety, 123–124
posttraumatic growth, 4
precuneus, 42–43
prefrontal cortex, 8–9, 11, 42,
101–103
priorities, 84–86
Prolonged Exposure therapy,
133–134
protective mechanisms, 138
Proust, Marcel, 152–154
psych ward, 19–23
PTSD, Prolonged Exposure
therapy for, 133–134

rage
shame and, 190–191, 197–198
simmering, 3, 125, 191,
218, 220
rebound effect, 130
reinforcement, positive, 206
reintegration, 34, 180
relabeling your files, 82–83

relational home, 12
relationships, 85
relief, joy as, 158
resistance to joy. *See* joy resistance
responsibility, promoted by
    guilt, 177
reverence, 52–59
Richie (client), 61–68, 73–75, 77,
    80–81, 89
rumination, 45, 52

sabotage, 19, 178, 195, 197, 199,
    201, 209
Sarah (client), 190–205, 208–209
scaling down
    joy, 25–29
    the scary, 202–205
schadenfreude, 160
schizophrenia, 120–121, 123
searching, 80, 82
secrecy, shame and, 190–191,
    203, 209
selective serotonin reuptake
    inhibitor (SSRI), 103
self-hatred/loathing, 191–192,
    194
self-referential thoughts, 40,
    42, 45
self-reflection, 42, 85
self-sabotage, 197, 201
self-worth, 18, 189, 196, 199, 201
sensory treasure map, 160–163
serotonin, 103, 131
shame. *See also* joy shame
    description, 18–19
    guilt difference from, 189–190
    as pack of thieves, 192–200
    rewiring your brain,
        200–202, 209

Sarah (client), 190–205,
    208–209
scaling down the scary,
    202–205
    unchecked, 209
    visceral, 189–190
simmering, 125
Sisyphus, 70–72
slut, shame from term,
    194–198, 203
snapback effect, 126–132,
    134, 139
social justice, influence of guilt
    on, 177
social norms, guilt as enforcement
    mechanism of, 175–176
Somatic Experiencing therapy, 133
sorrow, 154
spirituality, 55
SSRI (selective serotonin reuptake
    inhibitor), 103
stars, 213–214
Stevenson, Bryan, 169
stigma, of mental health care, 34
stress
    adaptation to, 132
    emotional numbing, 67
    joy as medicine for, 131–132
suicide
    Camus on, 72
    emotional, 67
    existentialism, 70, 72, 77
    taboo subject, 63
    thought of as adaptation, 70
    why?, 64
suicide attempts, 63–64, 81
supernova, 213–214
Swann's Way (Proust), 152–154
sympathetic nervous system, 131

taboo, of talking about suicide, 63
thieves, joy, 15–19, 29, 198–200, 214, 221
thinking, self-referential, 40, 42, 45
tiny gratitude acts, 107–109
tiny little joys (TLJs)
  exercise, 26–28
  imprinting, 23, 26, 28, 160
  practice described, 22–23
  redirecting guilt, 182–185
Tiny Little Joy Tracker, 27
tiny little mercies, 158, 160
titration, 133, 135–136, 139, 142
To the Lighthouse (Woolf), 155–158
toxic positivity, 29
transformation
  by awe, 59, 89
  of love, 107
  posttraumatic, 4
trauma
  childhood, 137
  default responses, 10–12
  definition, 12
  joy stolen by, 9–19
  Prolonged Exposure therapy, 133–134
  repetitive exposure to, 12

Somatic Experiencing therapy, 133
treasure map, sensory, 160–163
trigger
  description, 114–120
  joy as, 114, 120–126
TV analogy for DMN, 41, 45

values control panel, resetting your, 84–86
vigil, 87, 89
visual design, 55
Voltaire, 1
vulnerability
  avoiding, 132
  embracing, 113
  equating joy with, 137
  of joy, 127
  rage as armor, 197
  scaling down the scary, 202–205

Watson, John, 17, 119–120
wave machine, 132–135
Woolf, Virginia, 155–157
world building, 80–81, 86–89
worldview, 23, 39–41, 43, 160
worth, self-, 18, 189, 196, 199, 201
writing, free, 24–25

About the Author

Dr. MaryCatherine McDonald is a trauma researcher, author, and educator who has spent nearly two decades helping people reframe the way they understand grief, resilience, and joy. With a PhD in the philosophy of psychology and a knack for turning complex neurobiological concepts into practical tools, she's made it her mission to help people find light in the darkest moments.

Dr. McDonald has written four books along with many academic papers that nobody reads, delivered countless workshops, and created an online community where members geek out about trauma, joy, and the occasional weirdly insightful pop culture reference. She firmly believes that joy is not reserved for the perfect Pinterest moments but is often found in tiny, gritty, everyday experiences, like the quiet satisfaction of tiptoeing around a bookstore, or the unbridled thrill of reuniting with her movie-night crew for a nostalgic classic.

When she's not researching stress and trauma or teaching others how to rewire their brains, she's likely dancing in the kitchen, making cookies, or trying to steal someone else's dog on a hiking trail.